Dale in
Daily Life

Dale Harbison Carnegie was an American writer and the developer of famous courses in self-development, salesmanship, corporate training, public speaking, and interpersonal skills. He is the author of the bestselling *How to Win Friends and Influence People*, *How to Stop Worrying and Start Living*, and many more self-help books.

Dale in Daily Life

Applying *Carnegie's Wisdom*
in the *Modern World*

Dale Carnegie

RUPA

Published by
Rupa Publications India Pvt. Ltd 2024
7/16, Ansari Road, Daryaganj
New Delhi 110002

Sales centres:
Bengaluru Chennai
Hyderabad Jaipur Kathmandu
Kolkata Mumbai Prayagraj

Edition copyright © Rupa Publications India Pvt. Ltd 2024

All rights reserved.
No part of this publication may be reproduced, transmitted,
or stored in a retrieval system, in any form or by any means,
electronic, mechanical, photocopying, recording or otherwise, without
the prior permission of the publisher.

P-ISBN: 978-93-5702-913-1
E-ISBN: 978-93-5702-806-6

Second impression 2024

10 9 8 7 6 5 4 3 2

Printed in India

This book is sold subject to the condition that it shall not, by way of
trade or otherwise, be lent, resold, hired out, or otherwise circulated,
without the publisher's prior consent, in any form of binding or
cover other than that in which it is published.

CONTENTS

1. Find Yourself and Be Yourself: Remember There Is No One Else on Earth like You ... 7
2. Creating a Positive Mental Attitude ... 16
3. Develop Confidence ... 26
4. One of the Two Major Decisions of Your Life ... 41
5. Setting Goals ... 52
6. The Secret of Socrates ... 64
7. Listening to Learn ... 70
8. Respecting the Dignity of Others ... 82
9. Don't Try to Saw Sawdust ... 93
10. The High Road to Reason ... 100
11. Think Before You Criticise ... 106
12. If You're Wrong, Admit It ... 118
13. How to Analyse and Solve Worry Problems ... 124
14. Four Good Working Habits That Will Help Prevent Fatigue and Worry ... 132
15. Do This—and Criticism Can't Hurt You ... 138
16. Fool Things I Have Done ... 141
17. Remember That No One Ever Kicks a Dead Dog ... 145
18. Would You Take a Million Dollars for What You Have? ... 150
19. Eight Words That Can Transform Your Life ... 154

1

FIND YOURSELF AND BE YOURSELF: REMEMBER THERE IS NO ONE ELSE ON EARTH LIKE YOU

I have a letter from Mrs Edith Allred, of Mount Airy, North Carolina, 'As a child, I was extremely sensitive and shy,' she says in her letter. 'I was always overweight and my cheeks made me look even fatter than I was. I had an old-fashioned mother who thought it was foolish to make clothes look pretty. She always said, 'Wide will wear while narrow will tear', and she dressed me accordingly. I never went to parties; never had any fun; and when I went to school, I never joined the other children in outside activities, not even athletics. I was morbidly shy. I felt I was "different" from everybody else, and entirely undesirable.

'When I grew up, I married a man who was several years my senior. But I didn't change. My in-laws were a poised and self-confident family. They were everything I should have been but simply was not. I tried my best to be like them, but I couldn't. Every attempt they made to draw me out of myself only drove me further into my shell. I became nervous and irritable. I avoided all friends. I got so bad, I even dreaded the sound of the doorbell ringing! I was a failure. I knew it; and I was afraid my husband would find it out. So, whenever we were in public, I tried to be gay and overacted my part. I knew I overacted; and I would be miserable for days afterwards. At last I became so unhappy that I could see no point in prolonging my existence. I began to think of suicide.'

What happened to change this unhappy woman's life? Just a chance remark!

'A chance remark,' Mrs. Allred continued, 'transformed my whole life. My mother-in-law was talking one day of how she brought her children up, and she said, "No matter what happened, I always insisted on their being themselves." "On being them-selves." That remark is what did it! In a flash, I realized I had brought all this misery on myself by trying to fit myself into a pattern to which I did not conform.

'I changed overnight! I started being myself. I tried to make a study of my own personality. Tried to find out *what I was.* I studied my strong points. I learned all I could about colours and styles and dressed in a way that I felt was becoming to me. I reached out to make friends. I joined an organization—a small one at first—and was petrified with fright when they put me on a program. But each time I spoke, I gained a little courage. It took a long while—but today I have more happiness than I ever dreamed possible. In rearing my own children, I have always taught them the lesson I had to learn from such bitter experience: *no matter what happens, always be yourself!*'

'This problem of being willing to be yourself is as old as history,' says Dr. James Gordon Gilkey, 'and as universal as human life.' This problem of being unwilling to be yourself is the hidden spring behind many neuroses and psychoses and complexes. Angelo Patri has written thirteen books and thousands of syndicated newspaper articles on the subject of child training, and he says, 'Nobody is so miserable as he who longs to be somebody and something other than the person he is in body and mind.'

This craving to be something you are not is especially rampant in Hollywood. Sam Wood, one of Hollywood's best-known directors, says the greatest headache he has with aspiring young actors is exactly this problem: to make them be themselves. They all want to be second-rate Lana Turners or third-rate Clark Gables. 'The public has already had that flavour,' Sam Wood keeps telling them; 'now it wants something else.'

Before he started directing such pictures as *Goodbye, Mr Chips* and *For Whom the Bell Tolls,* Sam Wood spent years in the real-estate business, developing sales personalities. He declares that the same principles apply in the business world as in the world of moving pictures. You won't get anywhere playing the ape. You can't be a parrot. 'Experience has taught me,' says Sam Wood, 'that it is safest to drop, as quickly as possible, people who pretend to be what they aren't.'

I recently asked Paul Boynton, employment director for the Socony-Vacuum Oil Company, what is the biggest mistake people make in applying for jobs. He ought to know: he has interviewed more than sixty thousand job seekers; and he has written a book entitled *6 Ways to Get a Job*. He replied, 'The biggest mistake people make in applying for jobs is in not being themselves. Instead of taking their hair down and being completely frank, they often try to give you the answers they think you want.' But it doesn't work, because nobody wants a phony. Nobody ever wants a counterfeit coin.

A certain daughter of a streetcar conductor had to learn that lesson the hard way. She longed to be a singer. But her face was her misfortune. She had a large mouth and protruding buck teeth. When she first sang in public—in a New Jersey night club—she tried to pull down her upper lip to cover her teeth. She tried to act 'glamorous'. The result? She made herself ridiculous. She was headed for failure.

However, there was a man in this night club who heard the girl sing and thought she had talent. 'See here,' he said bluntly, 'I've been watching your performance and I know what it is you're trying to hide. You're ashamed of your teeth!' The girl was embarrassed, but the man continued, 'What of it? Is there any particular crime in having buck teeth? Don't try to hide them! Open your mouth, and the audience will love you when they see you're not ashamed. Besides,' he said shrewdly, 'those teeth you're trying to hide may make your fortune!'

Cass Daley took his advice and forgot about her teeth. From that time on, she thought only about her audience. She opened her mouth wide and sang with such gusto and enjoyment that she became a top star in movies and radio. Other comedians are now trying to copy *her!*

PURSUIT OF SELFHOOD

The renowned William James was speaking of men who had never found themselves when he declared that the average man develops only ten per cent of his latent mental abilities. 'Compared to what we ought to be,' he wrote, 'we are only half awake. We are making use of only a small part of our physical and mental resources. Stating the thing broadly, the human individual thus lives far within his limits. He possesses powers of various sorts which he habitually fails to use.'

You and I have such abilities, so let's not waste a second worrying because we are not like other people. You are something new in this world. Never before, since the beginning of time, has there ever been anybody exactly like you; and never again throughout all the ages to come will there ever be anybody exactly like you again. The new science of genetics informs us that you are what you are largely as a result of twenty-four chromosomes contributed by your father and twenty-four chromosomes contributed by your mother. These forty-eight chromosomes comprise everything that determines what you inherit. 'In each chromosome there may be,' says Amran Scheinfeld, 'anywhere from scores to hundreds of genes—with a single gene, in some cases, able to change the whole life of an individual.' Truly, we are 'fearfully and wonderfully' made.

Even after your mother and father met and mated, there was only one chance in 300,000 billion that the person who is specifically you would be born! In other words, if you had 300,000 billion brothers and sisters, they might have all been different from you. Is all this guesswork? No. It is a scientific fact. If you would like to read more about it, go to your public library and borrow a book entitled *You and Heredity* by Amran Scheinfeld.

I can talk with conviction about this subject of being yourself because I feel deeply about it. I know what I am talking about. I know from bitter and costly experience. To illustrate: when I first came to New York from the cornfields of Missouri, I enrolled in the American Academy of Dramatic Arts. I aspired to be an actor. I had what I thought was a brilliant idea, a short cut to success, an idea so simple, so fool proof, that I couldn't understand why thousands of ambitious people hadn't already discovered it. It was this: I would study how the famous actors of that day—John Drew, Walter Hampden, and Otis Skinner—got their effects. Then I would imitate the best points of each one of them and make myself into a shining, triumphant combination of all of them. How silly! How absurd! I had to waste years of my life imitating other people before it penetrated through my thick Missouri skull that I had to be myself, and that I couldn't possibly be anyone else.

That distressing experience ought to have taught me a lasting lesson. But it didn't. Not me. I was too dumb. I had to learn it all over again. Several years later, I set out to write what I hoped would be the best book on public speaking for businessmen that had ever been written. I had the same foolish idea about writing this book that I had formerly had about acting: I was going to *borrow* the ideas of a lot of other writers and put them all in one book—a book that would have everything. So I got scores of books on public speaking and spent a year incorporating their ideas into my manuscript. But it finally dawned on me once again that I was playing the fool. This hodgepodge of other men's ideas that I had written was so synthetic, so dull, that no businessman would ever plod through it. So I tossed a year's work into the wastebasket, and started all over again. This time I said to myself, 'You've got to be Dale Carnegie, with all his faults and limitations. You can't possibly be anybody else.' So I quit trying to be a combination of other men, and rolled up my sleeves and did what I should have done in the first place: I wrote a textbook on public speaking out of my own experiences, observations and convictions as a speaker and a teacher of speaking. I learned—for all time, I hope—the lesson that Sir Walter Raleigh learned. (I am *not* talking about the Sir Walter who threw his coat in the mud for the Queen to step on. I am talking about the Sir Walter Raleigh who was professor of English literature at Oxford back in 1904.) 'I can't write a book commensurate with Shakespeare,' he said, 'but I can write a book by me.'

Be yourself. Act on the sage advice that Irving Berlin gave the late George Gershwin. When Berlin and Gershwin first met, Berlin was famous but Gershwin was a struggling young composer working for thirty-five dollars a week in Tin Pan Alley. Berlin, impressed by Gershwin's ability, offered Gershwin a job as his musical secretary at almost three times the salary he was then getting. 'But don't take the job,' Berlin advised. 'If you do, you may develop into a second-rate Berlin. But if you insist on being yourself, someday you'll become a first-rate Gershwin.'

Gershwin heeded that warning and slowly transformed himself into one of the significant American composers of his generation.

Charlie Chaplin, Will Rogers, Mary Margaret McBride, Gene Autry and millions of others had to learn the lesson I am trying to hammer home in this chapter. They had to learn the hard way—just as I did.

When Charlie Chaplin first started making films, the director of the pictures insisted on Chaplin's imitating a popular German comedian of that day. Charlie Chaplin got nowhere until he acted himself. Bob Hope had a similar experience: spent years in a singing-and-dancing act—and got nowhere until he began to wisecrack and be himself. Will Rogers twirled a rope in vaudeville for years without saying a word. He got nowhere until he discovered his unique gift for humour and began to talk as he twirled his rope.

When Mary Margaret McBride first went on the air, she tried to be an Irish comedian and failed. When she tried to be just what she was—a plain country girl from Missouri—she became one of the most popular radio stars in New York.

When Gene Autry tried to get rid of his Texas accent and dressed like city boys and claimed he was from New York, people merely laughed behind his back. But when he started twanging his banjo and singing cowboy ballads, Gene Autry started out on a career that made him the world's most popular cowboy, both in pictures and on the radio.

You are something new in this world. Be glad of it. Make the most of what nature gave you. In the last analysis, all art is autobiographical. You can sing only what you are. You can paint only what you are. You must be what your experiences, your environment and your heredity have made you. For better or for worse, you must cultivate your own little garden. For better or for worse, you must play your own little instrument in the orchestra of life.

As Emerson said in his essay on 'Self-Reliance': 'There is a time in every man's education when he arrives at the conviction that envy is ignorance; that imitation is suicide; that he must take himself for better, for worse, as his portion; that though the wide universe is full of good, no kernel of nourishing corn can come to him but through his toil bestowed on that plot of ground which is given him to till. The power which resides in him is new in nature, and none but he knows what that is which he can do, nor does he know until he has tried.'

That is the way Emerson said it. But here is the way a poet—the late Douglas Malloch—said it:

'If you can't be a pine on the top of the hill,
Be a scrub in the valley—but be the best little scrub by the side of the rill;
Be a bush, if you can't be a tree.
If you can't be a bush, be a bit of the grass,
And some highway happier make;
If you can't be a muskie, then just be a bass—
But the liveliest bass in the lake!
We can't all be captains, we've got to be crew,
There's something for all of us here.

There's big work to do and there's lesser to do,
And the task we must do is the near.
If you can't be a highway, then just be a trail,
If you can't be the sun, be a star;
It isn't by size that you win or you fail—
Be the best of whatever you are!'

POINTS TO REMEMBER:

1. No matter what happens, always be yourself!
2. Stop imitating others.
3. Do not waste a second worrying because you are not like other people. You are something new in this world.

2

CREATING A POSITIVE MENTAL ATTITUDE

Monsignor Tom Hartman has been a priest for more than twenty years. His whole life is dedicated to the service of God and others. His days consist of consoling the needy, ministering to the sick, advising the distraught and trying to bring people closer to God. But one thing was sadly missing from the monsignor's busy days.

One morning his father phoned at the rectory. In those days Hartman was assigned to St. James Parish in Seaford, Long Island. His father owned a liquor store down the road in Farmingdale. In all his years of growing up and in all his time as a priest, Hartman could never remember his parents saying anything negative about him. But on the phone that morning, his father's voice had a slightly irritated tone.

'Tom, I'd like to sit down and talk with you about something,' his father said.

'Sure,' Hartman told him, and the two men made a date.

When they finally got together, his father spoke immediately about what was on his mind. 'Tom,' he said, 'your mother and I admire you. We're always hearing about the good work you are doing, and we're very proud of you. But I think you're overlooking your family. I understand you've got to help a lot of people in your life, but many of those people are going to come and go. Your family will always be there for you. And what's happened is, when you call us, you're always asking us to do something for you. You just seem too busy to take the time to talk.'

Hartman was momentarily taken aback. 'Well, Dad,' he said, 'when I was growing up, I watched you. You were in the produce business working seventy hours a week. And I have to say I admired you. So you know, I've tried to do the same.'

But his father didn't sound convinced. 'What you don't see, Tom, is that your work is harder than mine was,' he said. 'Mine was physical. It was fruit and produce. And then I would come home and be present with my family.' Hartman didn't know what to say, and he felt relieved when his father said he wasn't really looking for any instant response. 'I just want you to think about this,' his father said.

Hartman was disturbed enough by the conversation to cancel the rest of his appointments for the day. Then he decided to call his brothers and sisters. He described later what he discovered on the phone. 'When I called them,' he said, 'we were into the conversation about three or four minutes, and every one of them said almost the exact same thing, "What do you want?" That's when I had to admit that my father was right.'

Even a man whose calling is to maintain perspective and balance needed to have someone remind him that—in one part of his life, at least—he wasn't practicing what he preached. That's a mistake everyone makes from time to time.

ADOPT A HEALTHY LIFESTYLE

It is vital for all of us to balance out our lives, to make room for things other than work. This won't only produce happier and more satisfying personal lives. Almost inevitably, it will also make people more energetic, more focused and more productive at work.

Walter A. Green, the chairman of Harrison Conference Services, likens a balanced, productive life to a 'several-legged stool'. Too many people, Green believes, have only a single dimension to their lives. They are focused round the clock on their careers.

'In my experience, all too often, this one-dimensional perspective continues throughout one's life,' Green says. 'What I would urge is that your life be a several-legged stool, with a dimension for your family, another for your friends, your avocations, your health. I have seen many examples of people in their thirties, forties and fifties whose professions or careers did not materialize as they had expected. This spells trouble for those whose lives have been a one-legged stool.'

This is a problem even for highly successful people. 'At some stage in your life,' Green continues, 'you will want something else. It is possible to begin to develop friendships and interests after middle age. But watch a fifty-year-old learn to ride a bicycle for the first time!' It's not a graceful sight.

The importance of balance—to individuals and to the companies that employ them—is only now being fully understood. But well-led companies everywhere are trying to help their people put true balance into their lives.

At the New York City headquarters of Tiger Management Corporation, a worldwide money-management firm, a fully equipped workout room has been installed right outside the president's office. All Tiger employees are encouraged to use it.

'The gym is going to be tripled in size,' Tiger President Julian H. Robertson, Jr., says proudly. 'I find the young people all seem to come here after work. The fact that they are here rather than at health clubs all over the city is a tremendous boon for us. They are talking with each other. They are exchanging ideas. All that is really good for us.' And obviously it's good for them too—physically and mentally.

'I don't think it's possible to be a great manager or a great executive without being a total person,' says Andrés Navarro, president of SONDA, S.A., a Chilean computer-systems company that does business in North and South America. Navarro has an apt analogy. 'If you want to be an athlete, maybe to throw the javelin, it's not enough to have the strongest arm. You need the whole body to be strong.

And if you want to be a great leader, you need all parts of your life to be strong and intact. 'You see,' explains Navarro, 'a good executive who makes great decisions and makes money in the company but doesn't get along with his wife, his children and other people in general is missing a crucial part of life. If you want to grow and be a good leader, you've got to be a complete man—or a complete woman. And the most important part of it is your family.'

Richard Fenstermacher of the Ford Motor Company promotes the very same idea among his employees. 'We tell our people, "Your lives are two-dimensional,"' Fenstermacher says. 'If you find all of your identity at Ford, that's going to be a problem because you have a responsibility to your family as well.'

Undeniably, most modern leaders don't achieve a perfect balance all of the time. The many balls that are being juggled aren't easy to keep aloft. The usual tendency for ambitious people is to put the business first. It just seems so much more urgent, so much more pressing, so much more crucial.

Fred Sievert at New York Life has a different set of pressures on his time, but he admits candidly that he too finds it hard to manage all the competing interests in his life. 'I'm struggling every day to bring balance into my life,' he says. 'I could literally spend all my waking hours at work and a year from now not know everything I'd like to know. It's very difficult.'

Yes, it is. Attaining a reasonable division of time between work and leisure 'is the greatest challenge,' believes Ray Stata, of Analog Devices, Inc. But it's worth the effort to master the challenge.

John B. Robinson, Jr., of Fleet Financial Group, Inc., has realized the benefits that come with having a happy home life. 'There has never been any doubt in my mind what's most important to me,' says Robinson. A big title? Salary? Stock options? A country home? 'What's most important to me, long-term, is myself, my wife and my family.' What does this mean in practice? 'I try to keep a sense of what's fair and what's equitable, and if I've been giving too much to the job and not enough to the family, I say, "I'm not going to do that. I'm not going to say yes to that dinner, and I'm not going to short-change my family life."'

Most people, if they were asked directly, would probably echo Robinson's sentiments. Family is more important. Time to play is essential. But most people don't put that concept into action. They don't treat balance as a top priority. They fall into the habit of responding to the immediate pressure of work and ignoring the immediate and long-term pleasure that flows from having a satisfying personal life.

After his revelation about his family life, Monsignor Tom Hartman taught himself how to 'waste' time. 'I try in my life for an hour a day to do nothing,' Hartman explains. 'I waste time with God, with people, with nature, my job. It has transformed my eyes. Now I see the connection we have to each other. It is so important not to force things but to appreciate them.' Appreciate your family, your friends, your environment, yourself, whatever it is that gets your mind off work.

At Michael and Nancy Crom's home outside San Diego, Saturdays are always reserved for that. As Nancy grabs a few last minutes of sleep, Michael and daughter Nicole make pancakes, Nicole's favourite meal. The two of them go out to the garden, where they check on the strawberry plants, water the flowers and feed the birds. He tells her stories from the life of Nicky-Nicole and Belinda McIntosh, the make-believe characters the two of them have invented.

'We do that every Saturday, whether I've been traveling or I've been in the office,' Michael says. 'Watching the joy in her eyes keeps me joyful too.'

Wolfgang Schmitt of Rubbermaid takes a walk with his family most nights. 'It would be unusual if we didn't go out for a walk,' Schmitt explains. 'If our older sons are there, they go with us. The little guy always goes with us because he lives at home. We go out for forty minutes, an hour, whatever, just walking around. We do it no matter what the weather.'

Schmitt also makes a point of spending time alone. 'Just physically doing something is therapy. Raking leaves, cutting wood, planting trees. Any chore is therapeutic.'

Bill Makahilahila at SGS-Thomson makes time for himself every day—even though it means getting up at three o'clock in the morning. Makahilahila explains his practice of predawn rising: 'I'm busy all day. I'm usually here until seven or eight in the evening, and I know I need to be here in the morning. I don't know why, but I've just gotten to the point where I am in deep meditation in the mornings. It's so quiet, I can stretch myself, be creative, read or reflect on my day.'

The benefits are immediate. 'When I've done that,' he says, 'I begin to have peace of mind and self-confidence, even in the midst of the deepest problems that I know I'm going to have to face that day.'

Corning's David Luther runs. He also vacations with his wife and son four times a year, skiing or beachcombing. He makes sure he reads things that have nothing to do with work, and when all else fails, 'I just go out and sit on the deck and watch the hawks.'

Once you've analysed how to enjoy your leisure time, bring some of that same spirit into work. Who ever said the office has to be a depressing place?

Certainly not Richard Fenstermacher of the Ford Motor Company. Fenstermacher recalls doing business with a company that brought that spirit of levity right into the executive suite.

'When they bring somebody on the board,' explains Fenstermacher, 'they give the new person a Mickey Mouse watch. There's a big presentation out of the office. Everybody comes and stands around and somebody gives a speech. The thing is, you don't have to spend twenty-five years with this company to get a watch. Here's your watch. When you look at that watch, we want to remind you to have fun when you work. That's why it's Mickey Mouse.'

Tom Saunders makes enjoyment a high priority at his international merchant bank, Saunders Karp & Company. 'We waste time. When we've got a little bit of time to sit around, we laugh at each other about something or make fun of each other. I make fun of them all the time and they make fun of me worse. But all the time I'm ragging them, all the time. We have good times. We don't take ourselves too seriously.'

Television newsman Hugh Downs has borrowed Churchill's time-tested method of workday relaxation and given it his own special spin. 'The one thing I have in common with great people—only one thing—is that I can sleep for very short periods and be refreshed,' says Downs. 'I can sit down in a chair and go to sleep for three minutes, five minutes, and wake up and it's like I've had a night's sleep. I would go into my dressing room often when I was otherwise all ready and say, "Wake me two minutes before air time," And they'd come in and wake me two minutes before air. I'd go out and do the show.

'My wife laughs at that,' Downs continues. 'She says, "If you were condemned to death in two hours, you're going before the firing squad in two hours, you'd take a nap the first hour and face the problem the second hour." It's probably true. If there were nothing I could do about it in that first hour, it would be appropriate to take a nap.'

ENJOY THE CLIMB BEFORE THE MOUNTAIN TOP

What is always appropriate—at the office, at home, on the road, wherever you happen to find yourself—is to keep real balance in your life. As Fleet Financial's John Robinson says, 'There are many ways of getting involved in outside activities. Every time you get involved in outside interests, it adds balance—whether it's church-related, civic-related or school-related. I just try to avoid extremes, I guess.'

Singer-songwriter Neil Sedaka had two close friends growing up in Brooklyn, a young couple who had great ambition in their lives but also just loved to have a good time. Over the years they both achieved tremendous professional and financial success, but they lost something along the way. It was the balance they once knew in their lives. Sedaka wrote a song about his friends, which turned into a giant hit. The song was called 'The Hungry Years'.

'They struggled to hit the top,' Sedaka recalls. 'Success and money. But when they finally did it, they discovered that they missed the times when they were just getting started, when they were hanging out in the old neighbourhood, when they were building a life together.

'It's like, "I want that five-million-dollar home." But then you finally hit it, you actually get to move in and after a couple of months, you say, "Is this all? Is this it?" You miss those years that you did things together. You've lost some of the pleasure and balance in your life.' There's nothing wrong with material success, but that alone is not enough to sustain a happy life.

How can you start balancing your life? The first step is to change your attitude. You've got to stop thinking of time for your family, for exercise, or for leisure as wasted time. Achievers often feel they need to apologize for leisure time. Try to rid yourself of that thought. Relaxation is not a dirty word.

This leads to the second step in the process: you have to make time for leisure activity. Most of us are overcommitted. Perhaps it's time to re-evaluate priorities. Make a decision to devote as much energy to planning your leisure time as you devote to planning your workday.

The third step is to act. Do something. Get involved in activities that are not work-related. They will leave you happier, healthier, more focused and, as a result, a better leader.

CONSISTENTLY HIGH PERFORMANCE COMES FROM A BALANCE BETWEEN WORK AND LEISURE.

> **POINTS TO REMEMBER:**
> 1. Attaining a balanced life is more productive and satisfying.
> 2. Only a good person can be a good leader.
> 3. Achieving a reasonable balance between work and leisure is the greatest challenge.

3

DEVELOP CONFIDENCE

'There are always three speeches, for every one you actually gave. The one you practiced, the one you gave and the one you wish you gave.'

'Five years ago, Mr. Carnegie, I came to the hotel where you were conducting one of your demonstrations. I walked up to the door of the meeting room and then stopped. I knew if I entered that room and joined a class, sooner or later I'd have to make a speech. My hand froze on the doorknob. I couldn't go in. I turned my back and walked out of the hotel.

'If I had only known then how you make it easy to conquer fear, the paralysing fear of an audience, I wouldn't have lost these past five years.'

The man who spoke these revealing words wasn't talking across a table or a desk. He was directing his remarks to an audience of some two hundred people. It was the graduation session of one of my courses in New York City. As he gave his talk, I was particularly impressed by his poise and self-assurance. Here was a man, I thought, whose executive skills will be tremendously increased by his newly acquired expressiveness and confidence. As his instructor, I was delighted to see that he had dealt a death blow to fear and I couldn't help thinking how much more successful, and what is more, how much happier this man would have been if his victory over fear had come five or ten years before.

Emerson said, 'Fear defeats more people than any other one thing in the world.' Oh, how I have been made aware of the bitter truth of that statement. And how grateful I am that during my life I have been able to rescue people from fear. When I started to teach my course in 1912, little did I realize that this training would prove to be one of the best methods ever yet devised to help people eliminate their fears and feelings of inferiority. I found that learning to speak in public is nature's own method of overcoming self-consciousness and building up courage and self-confidence. Why? Because speaking in public makes us come to grips with our fears.

In years of training men and women to speak in public, I have picked up some ideas to help you quickly overcome stage fright and develop confidence in a few short weeks of practice.

FIRST
GET THE FACTS ABOUT FEAR OF SPEAKING IN PUBLIC

You are not unique in your fear of speaking in public. Surveys in colleges indicate that 80 to 90 per cent of all students enrolled in speech classes suffer from stage fright at the beginning of the course. I am inclined to believe that the figure is higher among adults at the start of my course, almost one hundred per cent.

A certain amount of stage fright is useful! It is nature's way of preparing us to meet unusual challenges in our environment. So, when you notice your pulse beating faster and your respiration speeding up, don't become alarmed. Your body, ever alert to external stimuli, is getting ready to go into action.

If these physiological preparations are held within limits, you will be capable of thinking faster, talking more fluently and generally speaking with greater intensity than under normal circumstances.

Many professional speakers have assured me that they never completely lose all stage fright. It is almost always present just before they speak, and it may persist through the first few sentences of their talk. This is the price these men and women pay for being like race horses and not like draft horses. Speakers who say they are 'cool as a cucumber' at all times are usually as thick-skinned as a cucumber and about as inspiring as a cucumber.

The chief cause of your fear of public speaking is simply that you are unaccustomed to speak in public. For most people, public speaking is an unknown quantity, and consequently one fraught with anxiety and fear factors. For the beginner, it is a complex series of strange situations, more involved than, say, learning to play tennis or drive a car. To make this fearful situation simple and easy: practice, practice, practice. You will find, as thousands upon thousands have, that public speaking can be made a joy instead of an agony merely by getting a record of successful speaking experiences behind you.

The story of how Albert Edward Wiggam, the prominent lecturer and popular psychologist, overcame his fear, has been an inspiration to me ever since I first read it. He tells how terror-struck he was at the thought of standing up in high school and delivering a five-minute declamation.

'As the day approached,' he writes, 'I became positively ill. Whenever the dreadful thought occurred to me, my whole head would flush with blood and my cheeks would burn so painfully that I would go out behind the school building and press them against the cold brick wall to try to reduce their surging blushes.

It was the same way with me in college.

'On one occasion, I carefully memorized a declamation beginning, "Adam and Jefferson are no more." When I faced the audience, my head was swimming so I scarcely knew where I was. I managed to gasp out the opening sentence, stating that, "Adams and Jefferson have passed away." I couldn't say another word, so I bowed...and walked solemnly back to my seat amid great applause. The president got up and said, "Well, Edward, we are shocked to hear the sad news, but we will do our best to bear up under the circumstances." During the uproarious laughter that followed, death would surely have been a welcome relief. I was ill for days afterward.

'Certainly, the last thing on earth I ever expected to become was a public speaker.'

A year after he left college, Albert Wiggam was in Denver. The political campaign of 1896 was raging over the issue of Free Silver. One day he read a pamphlet explaining the proposals of the Free Silverites; he became so incensed over what he considered the errors and hollow promises of Bryan and his followers, that he pawned his watch for enough money to get back to his native Indiana. Once there, he offered his services to speak on the subject of sound money. Many of his old school friends were in the audience. 'As I began,' he writes, 'the picture of my Adams and Jefferson speech in college swept over me. I choked and stammered and all seemed to be lost. But, as Chauncey Depew often said, both the audience and I managed somehow to live through the introduction; and encouraged by even this tiny success, I went on talking for what I thought was about fifteen minutes. To my amazement, I discovered I had been talking an hour and a half!

'As a result, within the next few years, I was the most surprised person in the world to find myself making my living as a professional public speaker.

'I knew at first-hand what William James meant by the habit of success.'

Yes, Albert Edward Wiggam learned that one of the surest ways of overcoming the devastating fear of speaking before groups is to get a record of successful experiences behind you.

You should expect a certain amount of fear as a natural adjunct of your desire to speak in public, and you should learn to depend on a limited amount of stage fright to help make you give a better talk.

If stage fright gets out of hand and seriously curtails your effectiveness by causing mental blocks, lack of fluency, uncontrollable tics and excessive muscular spasms, you should not despair. These symptoms are not unusual in beginners. If you make the effort, you will find the degree of stage fright soon reduced to the point where it will prove a help and not a hindrance.

SECOND
PREPARE IN THE PROPER WAY

The principal speaker at a New York Rotary Club luncheon several years ago was a prominent government official. We were looking forward to hearing him describe the activities of his department.

It was obvious almost at once that he had not planned his speech. At first he tried to talk impromptu. Failing in that attempt, he pulled out of his pocket a sheaf of notes which evidently had no more order than a flatcar full of scrap iron. He fumbled awhile with these, all the time becoming more embarrassed and inept in his delivery. Minute by minute he became more helpless, more bewildered. But he kept on floundering, apologizing, trying to make some semblance of sense out of his notes and raising a glass of water with a trembling hand to his parched lips. He was a sad picture of a man completely overcome by fright, due to almost total lack of preparation. He finally sat down, one of the most humiliated speakers I have ever seen. He made his talk as Rousseau says a love letter should be written: he began without knowing what he was going to say, and finished without knowing what he had said.

Since 1912, it has been my professional duty to evaluate over five thousand talks a year. From that experience, one great lesson stands out like Mount Everest, towering above all the others: *only the prepared speaker deserves to be confident.* How can anyone ever hope to storm the fortress of fear if he goes into battle with defective weapons, or with no ammunition at all? 'I believe,' said Lincoln, 'that I shall never be old enough to speak without embarrassment when I have nothing to say.'

If you want to develop confidence, why not do the one thing that will give you security as a speaker? 'Perfect love,' wrote the Apostle John, 'casteth out fear.' So does perfect preparation. Daniel Webster said he would as soon think of appearing before an audience half-clothed as half-prepared.

Never Memorize Word for Word. By 'perfect preparation' do I mean that you should memorize your talk? To this question I give back a thunderous NO. In their attempts to protect their egos from the dangers of drawing a mental blank before an audience, many speakers fall headlong into the trap of memorization. Once a victim of this type of mental dope addiction, the speaker is hopelessly bound to a time-consuming method of preparation that destroys effectiveness on the platform.

When H. V. Kaltenborn, the dean of American news commentators, was a student at Harvard University, he took part in a speech contest. He selected a short story entitled 'Gentlemen, the King'. He memorized it word for word and rehearsed it hundreds of times. The day of the contest he announced the title, 'Gentlemen, the King'. Then his mind went blank. It not only went blank; it went black. He was terrified. In desperation he started telling the story in his own words. He was the most surprised boy in the hall when the judges gave him first prize. From that day to this, H. V. Kaltenborn has never read nor memorized a speech. That has been the secret of success in his broadcasting career. He makes a few notes and talks naturally to his listeners without a script.

The man who writes out and memorizes his talks is wasting his time and energy, and courting disaster. All our lives we have been speaking spontaneously. We haven't been thinking of words. We have been thinking of ideas. If our ideas are clear, the words come as naturally and unconsciously as the air we breathe.

Even Winston Churchill had to learn that lesson the hard way. As a young man, Churchill wrote out and memorized his speeches. Then one day, while delivering a memorized talk before the British Parliament, he stopped dead in his mental tracks. His mind went blank. He was embarrassed, humiliated! He began his last sentence all over again. Again, his mind went blank and his face scarlet. He sat down. From that day to this, Winston Churchill has never attempted to deliver a memorized talk.

If we memorize our talk word for word, we will probably forget it when we face our listeners. Even if we do not forget our memorized talk, we will probably deliver it in a mechanical way. Why? Because it will not come from our hearts, but from our memories. When talking with people privately, we always think of something we want to say, and then we go ahead and say it without thinking of words. We have been doing that all our lives. Why attempt to change it now? If we do write out and memorize our talks, we may have the same experience that Vance Bushnell had.

Vance was a graduate of the Beaux Arts School in Paris, and later became vice-president of one of the largest insurance companies in the world—the Equitable Life Assurance Society. Years ago, he was asked to address a conference of two thousand Equitable Life representatives from all over America at a meeting in White Sulphur Springs, West Virginia. At that time, he had been in the life insurance business for only two years, but he had been highly successful, so he was scheduled to make a twenty-minute talk.

Vance was delighted to do so. He felt it would give him prestige. But unfortunately, he wrote out and memorized his talk. He rehearsed forty times in front of a mirror. He had everything down pat: every phrase, every gesture, every facial expression. It was flawless, he thought.

However, when he stood up to deliver his address, he was terrified. He said, 'My part in this program is....' His mind went blank. In his confusion, he took two steps backward and tried to start all over again. Again, his mind went blank. Again, he took two steps back and tried to start. He repeated this performance three times. The platform was four feet high; there was no railing at the back; and there was a space five feet wide between the back of the platform and the wall. So, the fourth time he stepped back, he toppled backwards off the platform and disappeared into space. The audience howled with laughter. One man fell off his chair and rolled in the aisle. Never before nor since in the history of the Equitable Life Assurance Society has anyone ever given such a comic performance. The astonishing part of the story is that the audience thought it was really an act. The old-timers of the Equitable Life are still talking about his performance.

But what about the speaker, Vance Bushnell? Vance Bushnell himself told me it was the most embarrassing occasion of his life. He felt so disgraced that he wrote out his resignation.

Vance Bushnell's superiors persuaded him to tear up his resignation. They restored his self-confidence; and Vance Bushnell, in later years, became one of the most effective speakers in his organization. But he never memorized a talk again. Let us profit by his experience.

I have heard countless scores of men and women try to deliver memorized talks, but I don't remember even one speaker who wouldn't have been more alive, more effective, more human, if he had tossed his memorized talk into the waste basket. If he had done that, he might have forgotten some of his points. He might have rambled, but at least he would have been human.

Abe Lincoln once said, 'I don't like to hear a cut-and-dried sermon. When I hear a man preach, I like to see him act as if he were fighting bees.' Lincoln said he wanted to hear a speaker cut loose and get excited. No speaker ever acts as if he were fighting bees when he is trying to recall memorized words.

Assemble and Arrange Your Ideas Beforehand. What, then, is the proper method of preparing a talk? Simply this: search your background for significant experiences that have taught you something about life, and assemble *your* thoughts, *your* ideas, *your* convictions, that have welled up from these experiences. True preparation means brooding over your topics. As Dr. Charles Reynold Brown said some years ago in a memorable series of lectures at Yale University, 'Brood over your topic until it becomes mellow and expansive…then put all these ideas down in writing, just a few words, enough to fix the idea…

put them down on scraps of paper—you will find it easier to arrange and organize these loose bits when you come to set your material in order.' This doesn't sound like such a difficult programme, does it? It isn't. It just requires a little concentration and thinking to a purpose.

Rehearse your talk. Should you rehearse your talk after you have it in some kind of order? By all means. Here is a sure-fire method that is easy and effective. Use the ideas you have selected for your talk in everyday conversation with your friends and business associates. Instead of going over the ball scores, just lean across the luncheon table and say something like this, 'You know, Joe, I had an unusual experience one day. I'd like to tell you about it.' Joe will probably be happy to listen to your story. Watch him for his reactions. Listen to his response. He may have an interesting idea that may be valuable. He won't know that you are rehearsing your talk, and it really doesn't matter. But he probably will say that he enjoyed the conversation.

Allan Nevins, the distinguished historian, gives similar advice to writer, 'Catch a friend who is interested in the subject and talk out what you have learned at length. In this way you discover facts of interpretation that you might have missed, points of arguments that had been unrealized, and the form most suitable for the story you have to tell.'

THIRD
PREDETERMINE YOUR MIND TO SUCCESS

In the first chapter, you remember, this sentence was used in reference to building the right attitude toward public speaking training in general. The same rule applies to the specific task now facing you, that of making each opportunity to speak a successful experience. There are three ways to accomplish this:

Lose Yourself in Your Subject. After you have selected your subject, arranged it according to plan and rehearsed it by 'talking it out' with your friends, your preparation is not ended. You must sell yourself on the importance of your subject. You must have the attitude that has inspired all the truly great personages of history—a belief in your cause. How do you fan the fires of faith in your message? By exploring all phases of your subject, grasping its deeper meanings and asking yourself how your talk will help the audience to be better people for having listened to you.

Keep Your Attention Off Negative Stimuli. For instance, thinking of yourself making errors of grammar or suddenly coming to an end of your talk somewhere in the middle of it is certainly a negative projection that could cancel confidence before you started. It is especially important to keep your attention off yourself just before your turn to speak. Concentrate on what the other speakers are saying, give them your wholehearted attention and you will not be able to work up excessive stage fright.

Give Yourself a Pep Talk. Unless he is consumed by some great cause to which he has dedicated his life, every speaker will experience moments of doubt about his subject matter. He will ask himself whether the topic is the right one for him, whether the audience will be interested in it. He will be sorely tempted to change his subject. At times like these, when negativism is most likely to tear down self-confidence completely, you should give yourself a pep talk. In clear, straightforward terms tell yourself that your talk is the right one for you, because it comes out of your experience, out of your thinking about life. Say to yourself that you are more qualified than any member of the audience to give this particular talk and, by George, you are going to do your best to put it across. Is this old-fashioned Coué teaching? It may be, but modern experimental psychologists now agree that motivation based on autosuggestion is one of the strongest incentives to rapid learning, even when simulated. How much more powerful, then, will be the effect of a sincere pep talk based on the truth?

FOURTH
ACT CONFIDENT

The most famous psychologist that America has produced, Professor William James, wrote, 'Action seems to follow feeling, but really action and feeling go together; and by regulating the action, which is under the more direct control of the will, we can indirectly regulate the feeling, which is not.

'Thus the sovereign voluntary path to cheerfulness, if our spontaneous cheerfulness be lost, is to sit up cheerfully and to act and speak as if cheerfulness were already there. If such conduct does not make you feel cheerful, nothing else on that occasion can.

'So, to feel brave, act as if we were brave, use all of our will to that end, and a courage-fit will very likely replace the fit of fear.'

Apply Professor James' advice. To develop courage when you are facing an audience, act as if you already had it. Of course, unless you are prepared, all the acting in the world will avail but little. But granted that you know what you are going to talk about, step out briskly and take a deep breath. In fact, breathe deeply for thirty seconds before you ever face your audience. The increased supply of oxygen will buoy you up and give you courage. The great tenor, Jean de Reszke, used to say that when you had your breath so you 'could sit on it', nervousness vanished.

Draw yourself up to your full height, look your audience straight in the eyes and begin to talk as confidently as if every one of them owed you money. Imagine that they do. Imagine that they have assembled there to beg you for an extension of credit. The psychological effect on you will be beneficial.

If you doubt that this philosophy makes sense, take the word of an American who will always be a symbol of courage. Once he was the most timorous of men; by practicing self-assurance, he became one of the boldest; he was the trust-busting, audience-swaying, Big-Stick-wielding President of the United States, Theodore Roosevelt.

'Having been a rather sickly and awkward boy,' he confesses in his autobiography, 'I was, as a young man, at the first both nervous and distrustful of my powers. I had to train myself painfully and laboriously not merely as regards my body but as regards my soul and spirit.'

Fortunately, he has disclosed how he achieved the transformation. 'When a boy,' he wrote, 'I read a passage in one of Marryat's books which always impressed me. In this passage, the captain of some small British man-of-war is explaining to the hero how to acquire the quality of fearlessness. He says that at the outset almost every man is frightened when he goes into action, but that the course to follow is for the man to keep such a grip on himself that he can act just as if he were not frightened. After this is kept up long enough, it changes from pretence to reality, and the man does in very fact become fearless by sheer dint of practicing fearlessness when he does not feel it.

'This was the theory upon which I went. There were all kinds of things of which I was afraid at first, ranging from grizzly bears to "mean" horses and gunfighters; but by acting as if I were not afraid I gradually ceased to be afraid. Most men can have the same experience if they choose.'

Overcoming fear of public speaking has a tremendous transfer value to everything that we do. Those who answer this challenge find that they are better persons because of it. They find that their victory over fear of talking before groups has taken them out of themselves into a richer and fuller life.

A salesman wrote, 'After a few times on my feet before the class, I felt that I could tackle anyone. One morning I walked up to the door of a particularly tough purchasing agent, and before he could say, "No," I had my samples spread out on his desk, and he gave me one of the biggest orders I have ever received.'

A housewife told one of our representatives, 'I was afraid to invite the neighbours in for fear that I wouldn't be able to keep the conversation going. After taking a few sessions and getting up on my feet, I took the plunge and held my first party. It was a great success. I had no trouble stimulating the group along interesting lines of talk.'

At a graduating class, a clerk said, 'I was afraid of the customers, I gave them a feeling that I was apologetic. After speaking to the class a few times, I found that I was speaking up with more assurance and poise, I began to answer objections with authoritativeness. My sales went up forty-five per cent the first month after I started to speak to this class.'

They discovered that it was easy to conquer other fears and anxieties and to be successful where before they may have failed. You, too, will be able to meet the problems and conflicts of life with a new sense of mastery. What has been a series of insoluble situations can become a bright challenge to increased pleasure in living.

POINTS TO REMEMBER:

1. Stage fright is a part of public speaking that is felt by all. It is not just you.
2. Rise above rote memorization if you want to be taken seriously.
3. 'Fake it till you make it'- Apply the *confidence mantra*.

4

ONE OF THE TWO MAJOR DECISIONS OF YOUR LIFE

If you are under eighteen, you will probably soon be called upon to make the two most important decisions of your life—decisions that will profoundly alter all the days of your years; decisions that may have far-reaching effects upon your happiness, your income, your health; decisions that may make or break you.

What are these two tremendous decisions?

First: *How are you going to make a living?* Are you going to be a farmer, a mail carrier, a chemist, a forest ranger, a stenographer, a horse doctor, a college professor, or are you going to run a ham-burger stand?

Second: *Whom are you going to select to be the father or mother of your children?*

Both of those great decisions are frequently gambles. 'Every boy,' says Harry Emerson Fosdick in his book, *The Power to See It Through*, 'every boy is a gambler when he chooses a vocation. He must stake his life on it.'

How can you reduce the gamble in selecting a vocation? Read on; we will tell you as best we can. First, try, if possible, to find work that you enjoy. I once asked David M. Goodrich,

Chairman of the Board, B. F. Goodrich Company—tire manufacturers—what he considered the first requisite of success in business, and he replied, 'Having a good time at your work. If you enjoy what you are doing,' he said, 'you may work long hours, but it won't seem like work at all. It will seem like play.'

Edison was a good example of that. Edison—the unschooled newsboy who grew up to transform the industrial life of America—Edison, the man who often ate and slept in his laboratory and toiled there for eighteen hours a day. But it wasn't toil to him. 'I never did a day's work in my life,' he exclaimed. 'It was all fun.'

No wonder he succeeded!

I once heard Charles Schwab say much the same thing. He said, 'A man can succeed at almost anything for which he has unlimited enthusiasm.'

But how can you have enthusiasm for a job when you haven't the foggiest idea of what you want to do? Mrs Edna Kerr, who once hired thousands of employees for the Dupont Company, and is now assistant director of industrial relations for the American Home Products Company, once told me, "The greatest tragedy I know of is that so many young people never discover what they really want to do. I think no one else is so much to be pitied as the person who gets nothing at all out of his work but his pay.' Mrs Kerr reports that even college graduates come to her and say, 'I have a B.A. degree from Dartmouth (or an M.A. from Cornell). Have you some kind of work I can do for your firm?' They don't know themselves what they are able to do, or even what they would like to do. Is it any wonder that so many men and women who start out in life with competent minds and rosy dreams end up at forty in utter frustration and even with a nervous breakdown? In fact, finding the right occupation is important even for your health. When Dr. Raymond Pearl, of Johns Hopkins, made a study, together with some insurance companies, to discover the factors that make for a long life, he placed 'the right occupation' high on the list. He might have said, with Thomas Carlyle, 'Blessed is the man who has found his work. Let him ask no other blessedness.'

STOP PUTTING YOUR FUTURE AT STAKE!

I recently spent an evening with Paul W. Boynton, employment supervisor for the Socony-Vacuum Oil Company. During the last twenty years he has interviewed more than seventy-five thousand people looking for jobs, and has written a book entitled *6 Ways to Get a Job*. I asked him, 'What is the greatest mistake young people make today in looking for work?'

'They don't know what they want to do,' he said. 'It is perfectly appalling to realize that a man will give more thought to buying a suit of clothes that will wear out in a few years than he will give to choosing the career on which his whole future depends—on which his whole future happiness and peace of mind are based!'

And so what? What can you do about it? You can take advantage of a new profession called *vocational guidance*. It may help you—or harm you—depending on the ability and character of the counsellor you consult. This new profession isn't even within gunshot of perfection yet. It hasn't even reached the Model T stage. But it has a great future. How can you make use of this science? By finding out where, in your community, you can get vocational tests and vocational advice. All the larger cities and thousands of smaller communities throughout the United States have this kind of service. If you are a veteran, the Veterans Administration will tell you where to apply. If you're not a veteran, then ask your public library or your local board of education where you may get vocational guidance. Hundreds of high schools and colleges have vocational-guidance bureaus. If you live in the country, write to your State Supervisor, Occupational Information and Guidance Service, in care of your state capitol. Many states have supervisors to give this sort of advice. In addition to the public agencies, a number of nationwide organizations, such as the YMCA, YWCA, American Red Cross, B'nai B'rith, Boys' Clubs of America, Kiwanis Clubs and the Salvation Army, have counsellors to help you solve your vocational problems.

They can only suggest. You have to make the decisions. Remember that these counsellors are far from infallible. They don't always agree with one another. They sometimes make ridiculous mistakes. For example, a vocational-guidance counsellor advised one of my students to become a writer solely because she had a large vocabulary. How absurd! It isn't as simple as that. Good writing is the kind that transfers your thoughts and emotions to the reader—and to do that, you don't need a large vocabulary, but you do need ideas, experience, convictions and excitement. The vocational counsellor who advised this girl with a large vocabulary to become an author succeeded in doing only one thing: he turned an erstwhile happy stenographer into a frustrated, would-be novelist.

The point I am trying to make is that vocational-guidance experts, even as you and I, are not infallible. Perhaps you had better consult several of them—and then interpret their findings in the sunlight of common sense.

You may think it strange that I am including a chapter like this in a book devoted to worry. But it isn't strange at all, when you understand how many of our worries, regrets and frustrations are spawned by work we despise. Ask your father about it—or your neighbour or your boss. No less an intellectual giant than John Stuart Mill declared that industrial misfits are 'among the heaviest losses of society'. Yes, and among the unhappiest people on this earth are those same 'industrial misfits' who hate their daily work!

Do you know the kind of man who 'cracked up' in the Army? The man who was misplaced! I'm not talking about battle casualties, but about the men who cracked up in ordinary service. Dr. William Menninger, one of our greatest living psychiatrists, was in charge of the Army's neuropsychiatric division during the war, and he says, 'We learned much in the Army as to the importance of selection and of placement, of putting the right man in the right job... A conviction of the importance of the job at hand was extremely important. *Where a man had no interest, where he felt he was misplaced, where he thought he was not appreciated, where he believed his talents were being misused, invariably we found a potential if not an actual psychiatric casualty.*"

Yes—and for the same reasons, a man may 'crack up' in industry. If he despises his business, he can crack it up, too.

Take, for example, the case of Phil Johnson. Phil Johnson's father owned a laundry, so he gave his son a job, hoping the boy would work into the business. But Phil hated the laundry, so he dawdled, loafed, did what he had to do and not a lick more. Some days he was 'absent'. His father was so hurt to think he had a shiftless, ambitionless son that he was actually ashamed before his employees.

One day Phil Johnson told his father he wanted to be a mechanic—work in a machine shop. What? Go back to overalls? The old man was shocked. But Phil had his way. He worked in greasy dungarees. He did much harder work than was required at the laundry. He worked longer hours, and he whistled at his job! He took up engineering, learned about engines, puttered with machines—and when Philip Johnson died, in 1944, he was president of the Boeing Aircraft Company and was making the Flying Fortresses that helped to win the war! If he had stuck with the laundry, what would have happened to him and the laundry—especially after his father's death? My guess is he would have ruined the business—cracked it up and run it into the ground.

Even at the risk of starting family rows, I would like to say to young people: *Don't feel compelled to enter a business or trade just because your family wants you to do it!* Don't enter a career unless you want to do it! However, consider carefully the advice of your parents. They have probably lived twice as long as you have. They have gained the kind of wisdom that comes only from much experience and the passing of many years. But, in the last analysis, you are the one who has to make the final decision. You are the one who is going to be either happy or miserable at your work.

POINTS TO KEEP IN MIND BEFORE CHOOSING A CAREER

Now, having said this, let me give you the following suggestions—some of them warnings—about choosing your work:

Read and study the following five suggestions about selecting a vocational-guidance counsellor. These suggestions are right from the horse's mouth. They were made by one of America's leading vocational-guidance experts, Professor Harry Dexter Kitson.

'Don't go to anyone who tells you that he has a magic system that will indicate your "vocational aptitude". In this group are phrenologists, astrologers, "character analysts", handwriting experts. Their "systems" do not work.

'Don't go to anyone who tells you that he can give you a test that will indicate what occupation you should choose. Such a person violates the principle that a vocational counsellor must take into account the physical, social and economic conditions surrounding the counselee; and he should render his service in the light of the occupational opportunities open to the counselee.'

'Seek a vocational counsellor who has an adequate library of information about occupations and uses it in the counselling process.

'A thorough vocational-guidance service generally requires more than one interview.

'Never accept vocational guidance by mail.'

Keep out of businesses and professions that are already jam-packed and overflowing! There are more than twenty thousand different ways of making a living in America. Think of it! Over twenty thousand. But do young people know this? Not unless they hire a swami to gaze into a crystal ball. The result? In one school, two thirds of the boys confined their choices to five occupations—five out of twenty thousand—and four fifths of the girls did the same. Small wonder that a few businesses and professions are overcrowded—small wonder that insecurity, worry and 'anxiety neuroses' are rampant at times among the white-collar fraternity! Beware especially of trying to elbow your way into such overcrowded fields as law, journalism, radio, motion pictures and the 'glamour occupations'.

Stay out of activities where the chances are only one out of ten of your being able to make a living. As an example, take selling life insurance. Each year countless thousands of men—frequently unemployed men—start out trying to sell life insurance without bothering to find out in advance what is likely to happen to them! Here is *approximately what does happen*, according to Franklin L. Bettger, Real Estate Trust Building, Philadelphia. For twenty years Mr. Bettger was one of the outstandingly successful insurance salesmen in America. He declares that 90 per cent of the men who start selling life insurance get so heartsick and discouraged that they give it up within a year. Out of the ten who remain, one man will sell 90 per cent of all the insurance sold by the ten and the remaining nine men will sell only 10 per cent of the insurance. To put it another way: if you start selling life insurance, the chances are nine to one that you will fail and quit within twelve months; and the chances are only one in a hundred that you will make ten thousand a year out of it. Even if you remain at it, the chances are only one out of ten that you will be able to do anything more than barely scratch out a living.

Spend weeks—even months, if necessary—finding out all you can about an occupation before deciding to devote your life to it! How? By interviewing men and women who have already spent ten, twenty or forty years in that occupation.

These interviews may have a profound effect on your future. I know that from my own experience. When I was in my early twenties, I sought the vocational advice of two older men. As I look back now, I can see that those two interviews were turning points in my career. In fact, it would be difficult for me even to imagine what my life would have been like had I not had those two interviews.

How can you get these vocational-guidance interviews? To illustrate, let's suppose that you are thinking about studying to be an architect. Before you make your decision, you ought to spend weeks interviewing the architects in your city and in adjoining cities. You can get their names and addresses out of a classified telephone directory. You can call at their offices either with or without an appointment. If you wish to make an appointment, write them something like this:

> 'Won't you please do me a little favour? I want your advice. I am eighteen years old, and I am thinking about studying to be an architect. Before I make up my mind, I would like to ask your advice.
>
> If you are too busy to see me at your office, I would be most grateful if you would grant me the privilege of seeing you for half an hour at your home.
>
> Here is a list of questions I would like to ask you:
>
> If you had your life to live over, would you become an architect again?
>
> After you have sized me up, I want to ask you whether you think I have what it takes to succeed as an architect.
>
> Is the profession of architecture overcrowded?
>
> If I studied architecture for four years, would it be difficult for me to get a job? What kind of job would I have to take at first?
>
> If I had average ability, how much could I hope to earn during the first five years?
>
> What are the advantages and disadvantages of being an architect?
>
> If I were your son, would you advise me to become an architect?'

If you are timid, and hesitate to face a 'big shot' alone, here are two suggestions that will help.

First, get a lad of your own age to go with you. The two of you will bolster up one another's confidence. If you haven't someone of your own age to go with you, ask your father to go with you.

Second, remember that by asking his advice you are paying this man a compliment. He may feel flattered by your request. Remember that adults like to give advice to young men and women. The architect will probably enjoy the interview.

If you hesitate to write letters asking for an appointment, then go to a man's office without an appointment and tell him you would be most grateful if he would give you a bit of advice.

Suppose you call on five architects and they are all too busy to see you (which isn't likely), call on five more. Some of them will see you and give you priceless advice—advice that may save you years of lost time and heartbreak.

Remember that you are making one of the two most vital and far-reaching decisions of your life. So, take time to get the facts before you act. If you don't, you may spend half a lifetime regretting it.

If you can afford to do so, offer to pay a man for a half-hour of his time and advice.

Get over the mistaken belief that you are fitted for only a single occupation! Every normal person can succeed at a number of occupations, and every normal person would probably fail in many occupations. Take myself, for example: if I had studied and prepared myself for the following occupations, I believe I would have had a good chance of achieving some small measure of success—and also of enjoying my work. I refer to such occupations as farming, fruit growing, scientific agriculture, medicine, selling, advertising, editing a country newspaper, teaching and forestry. On the other hand, I am sure I would have been unhappy, and a failure, at bookkeeping, accounting, engineering, operating a hotel or a factory, architecture, all mechanical trades and hundreds of other activities.

POINTS TO REMEMBER:

1. A man can succeed at almost anything for which he has unlimited enthusiasm.
2. If you know what you want to do, you have already climbed half of the success ladder.
3. Think smartly and decide wisely. Your life depends on it.

5

SETTING GOALS

Mary Lou Retton was just a high-school sophomore from West Virginia, a state that had never once produced a world-class gymnast.

'I was a nobody,' she says, 'and I was number one in the state.' She was a tiny fourteen-year-old, performing at a competition in Reno, Nevada. That's the day the great Bela Karolyi, the Romanian gymnastics coach who had guided Nadia Comaneci to Olympic gold, walked up behind Mary Lou.

'He was the king of gymnastics,' Retton recalls. 'He came up to me. He tapped me on the shoulder. He's a big man—six-three or six-four. He came up to me and said, "Mary Lou," in that deep Romanian accent. "You come to me, and I will make you an Olympic champion."'

The first thought that went racing through Retton's mind was, 'Yeah, right. No way.'

But of all the gymnasts in that Nevada arena, Bela Karolyi had noticed her. 'So we sat down, and we talked,' Retton remembers. 'He talked with my parents and said, "Listen, there's no guarantee that Mary Lou will even make the Olympic team, but I think she's got the material that it takes."'

What a goal that was! Since early childhood she had harboured dreams about one day performing in the Olympics.

But hearing the words come out of the great man's mouth—as far as Retton was concerned—that set the goal in stone.

'It was a very big risk for me,' she says. 'I was going to be moving away from my family and my friends, living with a family I had never met before, training with girls I didn't know. It pumped me up so much. I was scared. I didn't know what to expect. But I was excited too. This man wanted to train me. Little me, from Fairmont, West Virginia. I had been picked out.'

And she wasn't about to let Karolyi down. It was two and a half years later that Mary Lou Retton, after a pair of perfect tens, won the Olympic gold medal in gymnastics for America—and with it a place in the hearts of people everywhere.

AIM, AND THEN SHOOT

Goals give us something to shoot for. They keep our efforts focused. They allow us to measure our success.

So set goals—goals that are challenging but also realistic, goals that are clear and measurable, goals for the short term and goals for the long term.

When you reach one goal, take a second to pat yourself on the back. Then move on to the next goal, emboldened, strengthened and energized by what you've already achieved.

Eugene Lang, a New York City philanthropist, was making a graduation speech to a sixth-grade class at PS 121. This class had a group of children with absolutely no hope of ever going to college. In fact, there was very little hope that most of these children would even graduate from high school. But at the end of the graduation speech, Lang made a stunning offer. 'For any of you who graduate from high school, I will ensure that funds are available for you to go to college,' he said.

Of the forty-eight students in that sixth-grade class that day, forty-four graduated from high school and forty-two went to college. To put that into perspective, remember that 40 percent of inner-city students never graduate from high school, let alone go to college.

That monetary offer alone wasn't enough to ensure such great success. Lang also made sure that the students got the support they needed along the way. They were monitored and counselled through their last six years of school. But that one challenging goal, clearly articulated and within the students' reach, gave them an opportunity to visualize a future they never thought was possible. And by visualizing it for themselves, they were able to make their dreams reality.

In the words of Harvey Mackay, the best-selling business author, 'A goal is a dream with a deadline.'

Howard Marguleas is the chairman of a produce company called Sun World, and he's one of California's new breed of growers. He got to be that way by setting and meeting goal after goal. For years Marguleas had watched as the agriculture business went up and down—fat times, lean times, as impossible to predict as they were to control. At least that's how everyone said the fruit-and-vegetable business worked.

But Marguleas had a goal: to develop new and unique kinds of produce that could withstand the shifts in the tides of consumer buying. 'This business is really no different from real estate,' Marguleas reasoned. 'When the market's down, unless you have something very highly, uniquely different, you're in serious trouble. Same thing in agriculture. If you're just another producer of lettuce, carrots or oranges, and you have nothing different from anyone else, you do well only if there's a short supply. If there's a large supply, you won't do well. And that's what we've tried to adjust to, to find the windows of opportunity that come with being different, a niche in the marketplace.'

That's where the idea of a better pepper came from. Yes, a better pepper. If he could develop a pepper that was tastier than the peppers that other people grew, Marguleas assured himself, wouldn't the grocers of America want to stock it in good times and in bad?

So he did it, giving birth to the Le Rouge Royal pepper. 'It's an elongated, three-lobe pepper,' Marguleas says. 'We were told, you know, "You have to have a bell pepper, a square-shaped pepper, to sell." But once we tasted this pepper—the colour, the flavour, everything about it—we knew we had something. We knew that if we promoted it properly and advertised and merchandised it and put a name on it, we could get people to eat it. And once they ate it, they were going to continue to buy it.'

What all this taught Marguleas is, 'Never cease to pursue the opportunity to seek something different. Don't be satisfied with what you're doing. Always try to seek a way and a method to improve upon what you're doing, even if it's considered contrary to the traditions of an industry.'

Those who fail to establish independent goals for themselves become, in Marguleas's word, the 'me-toos' of the world. The me-toos, the people who follow but don't lead, do fine when times are good. But when times get tough, they inevitably get left behind.

Marguleas had his finger on something there. People who set goals—challenging goals, but goals that are also achievable—are the ones with solid grips on their futures, the ones who end up accomplishing extraordinary things.

Reebok International, Ltd., the athletic-shoe company, set a major corporate goal for itself: get Shaquille O'Neal. The Orlando Magic star wasn't going to come easy. Lots of major companies were eager to hire him as their spokesman.

'It was a question of convincing him that we had the best commitment to him, that we were willing to do something to create for him a program that the next guy couldn't do,' says Paul Fireman, Reebok's chairman.

The whole company geared up. 'We created an ad campaign before he was here. We created it for him exclusively. We spent money to create it and we really put our effort in. We were just absolutely committed to getting him. We took a gamble. We took a risk. We spent the money, the time and the commitment.' Sometimes that's what setting goals is all about.

'It would have been a major confrontation emotionally if we had lost,' Fireman said. 'If we didn't go so far to get him here, we wouldn't have had the loss emotionally. But we wouldn't have had the player, either.'

Goals aren't important only for companies. They're the building blocks that successful careers are made of.

Jack Gallagher worked in the family tyre business, where he had held just about every job—accounting, bookkeeping, manufacturing and sales. All that experience in the tyre business taught him one thing for sure: he didn't want to work in the tyre business.

One day Gallagher ran into a high-school friend who was working as an assistant administrator at a local hospital. 'That's what I'd like to do,' Gallagher told himself. 'I'd love to help people. I'd love to have a big business, and I'd love to lead a group for the right things.' There were several giant hurdles between Jack Gallagher and a hospital administrator's job—a graduate degree in hospital administration, for one thing, and a job at a hospital, for another.

But Gallagher had his goal, and he got started jumping the hurdles right away.

He talked his way into Yale. He won a stipend from the Kellogg Foundation. He got a loan from a local bank. He worked nights in the business office of North Shore University Hospital. And after he got the graduate degree, he applied for an administrative residency at North Shore.

'I interviewed with Jack Hausman, the chairman of the hospital's board,' Gallagher recalls. 'I must have spent three minutes with him, and I sold him in three minutes. He asked me a funny question. He knew I was married and had three kids. He said, "How are you going to afford it?" They paid thirty-nine hundred for a resident then.'

Gallagher recalls how he responded, 'Look, Mr. Hausman, I thought it out a long time before I came to see you here. I had to have everything set so I could live during this residency and move into an administrative role after that.'

He had a goal. He planned every detail. He worked tirelessly toward them. He's North Shore's CEO today.

Singer-songwriter Neil Sedaka, whose pop-music career has spanned more than three decades, learned to set goals when he was just a kid. Sedaka grew up in a rough part of Brooklyn, and he was never one of the tough guys. His earliest goal was a perfectly understandable one: to be liked, and thereby stay alive, through high school.

'I wasn't a fighter,' Sedaka explained recently. 'So I had to be liked. I always wanted to be liked. You know how it is. You're always afraid of getting into a fight.' Anyway, young Neil came up with what turned out to be an ingenious method of achieving his personal goal—music.

'There was a sweetshop near Lincoln High School, and there was a jukebox in the back,' he recalled. 'All the tough kids, the leather-set kids, would hang out there, and they would listen to Elvis and Fats Domino. This was the beginning of rock and roll. So I wrote a rock-and-roll song, and I sang it, and then I was like a hero with those leather-set kids. They even let me into their part of the sweetshop.'

The point here isn't whether Sedaka should have cared about acceptance from the tough kids. These things can seem awfully important in the high-school years. But he knew instinctively how to reach these other people—and how to achieve what was important to him at the time. For Sedaka, that high-school goal turned into a lifelong career, and this early success gave him the confidence to shoot for the stars in the future.

ROME WASN'T BUILT IN A DAY

Much the same process unfolded in the early life of Arthur Ashe, the late tennis champion. Almost single-handedly, Ashe broke down the colour barrier in professional tennis, a game that until he came along had been almost exclusively white. In his later years, Ashe fought a valiant battle against the AIDS virus, raising consciousness about the disease on ghetto street corners and in townhouse drawing rooms. His was a life of setting and reaching goals. For Ashe it started when he was a youngster on a tennis court. That's where he learned about achievement, one goal at a time.

'Breaking through that barrier, where you have set a goal and you achieve that goal, it sort of codifies whatever budding self-confidence you might have had,' Ashe said in an interview for this book just before his death.

That's how Ashe operated until the day he died. He'd set a goal and when he'd met that goal, he'd set another one. Why? 'The self-confidence itself, I think, transforms the individual,' he explained. 'It also spills over into other areas of life. Not only do you feel confident in whatever you are expert at, but you probably feel generally self-confident that you can do some other things as well, applying the same principles maybe to another task or to another set of goals.'

The goals must be realistic, and they must be attainable. Don't make the mistake of thinking you should, or can, accomplish everything today. Maybe you can't reach the moon this year, so plan a shorter trip. Set an interim goal.

Following that incremental approach, Ashe put himself on the big-time tennis map. 'My early coaches,' explained Ashe, 'set out definite goals which I bought into. The goals were not necessarily winning tennis tournaments. The goals were just things that we saw as difficult, that would require some hard work and some planning. And there was sort of an implied reward out there if I achieved those goals. Again, the goal wasn't necessarily winning this tournament or that tournament. And so incrementally, before I knew it, after I attained these mini goals along the way, all of a sudden, "Hey, I'm close to the big prize here."'

That's how Ashe always approached tough tennis matches. 'In a tournament, you'd want to get to the quarterfinals. Or in a match, you would want to not miss a certain number of backhand passing shots. Or maybe you'd want to improve your stamina to a point where you're not going to get tired when the weather is too hot. Those are the sorts of goals that help take your general focus off that long-range, elusive goal—the goal of being number one or winning the whole tournament.'

Most big challenges are best faced with a series of interim goals. That's a far more encouraging process—far more motivating too.

Dr. James D. Watson, the director of the Cold Spring Harbour Laboratory, has been locked in a lifelong struggle to find the cure for cancer. Is that his only goal? Of course not.

That would be too discouraging for anyone to bear. Watson has laid out a series of incremental goals for himself and his laboratory colleagues, goals they are meeting every year on the road to the ultimate cure.

'There are so many different cancers,' explains Watson, who won a Nobel prize for discovering the structure of DNA. 'We're going to cure some of them. Hopefully, we'll cure more of them.

'But you've got to pick interim goals' he says. 'The goal is not to kill colon cancer tomorrow. It's to understand the disease. And there are many different steps. No one wants to be led into defeat. You get your happiness one small goal at a time.'

That's the way it works. Set little goals. Meet them. Set new, slightly larger goals. Meet them. Succeed.

Long before Lou Holtz became Notre Dame's head football coach, he wanted nothing more than to play the game himself. But when he went out for his high-school team, he weighed just 115 pounds.

Holtz knew this was far too small. Still, he desperately wanted to play, so he came up with a plan. He memorized all eleven positions on the team. That way, if any player got hurt, he was immediately prepared to rush onto the field. It gave him eleven chances instead of one.

'It's the same way in business today,' says writer Harvey Mackay. 'If you're working out here in the office, volunteer to learn the phone system. Volunteer to know what's going on in computers. If you're in sales, you want to know about computers.' That way, when opportunities appear, you'll have a much greater chance of seizing them. Set goals that make you more valuable to your team—as Lou Holtz did—or to your company.

The idea is to set goals and then strive to meet them. Sometimes you'll succeed on schedule, sometimes things will take longer to achieve than you thought and sometimes you won't attain what you thought you would. Some things just aren't meant to be. The point is to keep planning and plugging away. You'll get there, just watch.

As Scalamandré Silks' Adriana Bitter says, 'Maybe we set our goals too high sometimes and we don't always reach the top end, but we certainly can start climbing that ladder.'

Without specific goals it's far too easy just to drift, never really taking charge of your life. Time gets wasted because nothing has a sense of urgency. There's no deadline. Nothing has to be done *today*. It's possible to put off anything indefinitely. Goals are what can give us direction and keep us focused.

David Luther of Corning is acutely aware of this modern propensity toward aimlessness. He worries about how it might affect his own children at home. So he's constantly talking to them about goals.

'Sometimes,' he reminds them, 'we get caught up in things.' Easy to say, of course, but how to avoid this pitfall? 'The point,' according to Luther, 'is to know yourself. Think what it is that you know and want to do. Forget the money, for a moment anyway. When you get to be the age of your parents, what is it you want to be able to point to that met your expectation, that made a difference?'

How are intelligent goals created? Mostly they just take a little thought, but there are some useful techniques for getting the mind focused on the task. You might try asking yourself the same questions Luther urges his children to ask. 'Stand back and say, "What is it I really want to be? What kind of life do I really want to lead? Am I heading in the right direction now?"' That advice makes sense no matter how far along you are in your career.

Once you establish what your goals are, prioritize them.

Not everything can be done at once, so you've got to ask yourself, "Which comes first? What goal is most important to me now?" Then try organizing your time and energy to reflect those priorities. This, often, is the most challenging part.

To prioritize his goals, Ted Owen, publisher of the *San Diego Business Journal*, follows the advice he got from a psychologist friend. 'He told me to take a piece of paper and draw a line down the centre. On the left, put any number you want. I put ten. Put the top ten things that you want to accomplish in your life before you retire at whatever age that is, one hundred or sixty or fifty.

'Put down those ten things. So you want to have a good retirement program. You want to have a nice home. You want to have a happy marriage. You want to have good health. Whatever those ten are. Then over here on the other side, you take those ten and prioritize them. One of those ten becomes number one, and so on.'

Simplistic? Maybe. But helpful too. Through this process, Owen discovered some things about himself he never knew. 'I found out that a job, a well-paying, steady job, a job that makes me feel good, was about number seven.' Once you identify your own number one, two, three and seven, creating well-crafted goals becomes a whole lot easier.

It's fine if, over the years, those goals develop and change. 'Before I was married, I would come in on the weekends just to read the newspaper here,' says Dr. Ronald Evans, a research professor at the Salk Institute for Biological Studies. 'I had nothing else to do. I loved being in labs. It was sort of a home away from home. Research is addicting,' he observes. 'It's incredibly challenging and pushes your intellectual limits. You make discoveries, and there's nothing like it.'

But life changes, pressures change and goals should be

evaluated too. 'With a family now,' Evans goes on, 'it's been very difficult to change my habits, but I have. You just have to say you can't do everything.'

Corporations need goals as much as individuals do, and the same basic rules apply when companies begin defining theirs: make them clear, keep them basic and don't set too many at once.

The huge Motorola corporation was run, in one recent year, with just three specific goals, expressed in precise, mathematical terms: to 'continue 10-X improvement' every two years, to 'get the voice of' the customer, to 'cut business-process cycle time by factor 10' in five years.

Don't worry about what this language means. It may or may not apply at your company. What's important here is that the company has its goals. These goals are clearly understood within the company. The goals are challenging but attainable. Progress is easily measurable. And if these goals are achieved, the company will have done extraordinarily well.

Those three specific goals provide enough vision to run an entire company. Imagine what three equally clear, equally realistic goals can do for one person's life.

POINTS TO REMEMBER:

1. Set a goal and never lose sight of it.
2. Your goal should be realistic and achievable.
3. Surround yourself with people who will help you reach your goals.

6

THE SECRET OF SOCRATES

In talking with people, don't begin by discussing the things on which you differ. Begin by emphasising—and keep on emphasising—the things on which you agree. Keep emphasising, if possible, that you are both striving for the same end and that your only difference is one of method and not of purpose.

Get the other person saying, 'Yes, yes' at the outset. Keep your opponent, if possible, from saying, 'No.'

The skilful speaker gets, at the outset, a number of 'Yes' responses. This sets the psychological process of the listeners moving in the affirmative direction. It is like the movement of a billiard ball. Propel in one direction, and it takes some force to deflect it; far more force to send it back in the opposite direction.

The psychological patterns here are quite clear. When a person says, 'No', and really means it, he or she is doing far more than saying a word of two letters. The entire organism—glandular, nervous, muscular—gathers itself together into a condition of rejection. There is, usually in minute but sometimes in observable degree, a physical withdrawal or readiness for withdrawal. The whole neuromuscular system, in short, sets itself on guard against acceptance. When, to the contrary, a person says, 'Yes', none of the withdrawal activities takes place. The organism is in a forward-moving, accepting, open attitude. Hence the more 'yeses' we can, at the very outset, induce, the more likely we are to succeed in capturing the attention for our ultimate proposal.

It is a very simple technique—this 'yes' response. And yet, how much it is neglected! It often seems as if people get a sense of their own importance by antagonising others at the outset.

Get a student to say 'no' at the beginning, or a customer, child, husband or wife, and it takes the wisdom and the patience of angels to transform that bristling negative into an affirmative.

The use of this 'yes, yes' technique enabled James Eberson, who was a teller in the Greenwich Savings Bank, in New York City, to secure a prospective customer who might otherwise have been lost.

'This man came in to open an account,' said Mr Eberson, 'and I gave him our usual form to fill out. Some of the questions he answered willingly, but there were others he flatly refused to answer.

'Before I began the study of human relations, I would have told this prospective depositor that if he refused to give the bank this information, we should have to refuse to accept this account. I am ashamed that I have been guilty of doing that very thing in the past. Naturally, an ultimatum like that made me feel good. I had shown who was boss, that the bank's rules and regulations couldn't be flouted. But that sort of attitude certainly didn't give a feeling of welcome and importance to the man who had walked in to give us his patronage.

'I resolved this morning to use a little horse sense. I resolved not to talk about what the bank wanted but about what the customer wanted. And above all else, I was determined to get him saying 'yes, yes' from the very start. So I agreed with him.

I told him the information he refused to give was not absolutely necessary.

'"However," I said, "suppose you have money in this bank at your death. Wouldn't you like to have the bank transfer it to your next of kin, who is entitled to it according to law?"

'"Yes, of course," he replied.

'"Don't you think," I continued, "that it would be a good idea to give us the name of your next of kin so that, in the event of your death, we could carry out your wishes without error or delay?"

'Again he said, "Yes."

'The young man's attitude softened and changed when he realised that we weren't asking for this information for our sake but for his sake. Before leaving the bank, this young man not only gave me complete information about himself but he opened, at my suggestion, a trust account, naming his mother as the beneficiary for his account, and he had gladly answered all the questions concerning his mother also.

'I found that by getting him to say "yes, yes" from the outset, he forgot the issue at stake and was happy to do all the things I suggested.'

Joseph Allison, a sales representative for Westinghouse Electric Company, had this story to tell, 'There was a man in my territory that our company was most eager to sell to. My predecessor had called on him for ten years without selling anything. When I took over the territory, I called steadily for three years without getting an order. Finally, after thirteen years of calls and sales talk, we sold him a few motors. If these proved to be all right, an order for several hundred more would follow. Such was my expectation.

'Right? I knew they would be all right. So when I called three weeks later, I was in high spirits.

'The chief engineer greeted me with this shocking announcement, "Allison, I can't buy the remainder of the motors from you."

'"Why?" I asked in amazement. "Why?"

'"Because your motors are too hot. I can't put my hand on them."

'I knew it wouldn't do any good to argue. I had tried that sort of thing too long. So I thought of getting the "yes, yes" response.

'"Well, now look, Mr Smith," I said. "I agree with you a hundred per cent; if those motors are running too hot, you ought not to buy any more of them. You must have motors that won't run any hotter than standards set by the National Electrical Manufacturers Association. Isn't that so?"

'He agreed it was. I had gotten my first "yes."

'"The Electrical Manufacturers Association regulations say that a properly designed motor may have a temperature of 72 degrees Fahrenheit above room temperature. Is that correct?"

'"Yes," he agreed. "That's quite correct. But your motors are much hotter."

'I didn't argue with him. I merely asked, "How hot is the mill room?"

'"Oh," he said, "about 75 degrees Fahrenheit."

'"Well," I replied, "if the mill room is 75 degrees and you add 72 to that, that makes a total of 147 degrees Fahrenheit. Wouldn't you scald your hand if you held it under a spigot of hot water at a temperature of 147 degrees Fahrenheit?"

'Again he had to say "yes."

'"Well," I suggested, "wouldn't it be a good idea to keep your hands off those motors?"

'"Well, I guess you're right," he admitted. We continued to chat for a while. Then he called his secretary and lined up approximately $35,000 worth of business for the ensuing month.

'It took me years and cost me countless thousands of dollars in lost business before I finally learned that it doesn't pay to argue, that it is much more profitable and much more interesting to look at things from the other person's viewpoint and try to get that person saying "yes, yes."'

Eddie Snow, who sponsors our courses in Oakland, California, tells how he became a good customer of a shop because the proprietor got him to say 'yes, yes'. Eddie had become interested in bow hunting and had spent considerable money in purchasing equipment and supplies from a local bow store. When his brother was visiting him he wanted to rent a bow for him from this store. The sales clerk told him they didn't rent bows, so Eddie phoned another bow store. Eddie described what happened:

'A very pleasant gentleman answered the phone. His response to my question for a rental was completely different from the other place. He said he was sorry but they no longer rented bows because they couldn't afford to do so. He then asked me if I had rented before. I replied, "Yes, several years ago." He reminded me that I probably paid $25 to $30 for the rental. I said "yes" again. He then asked if I was the kind of person who liked to save money. Naturally, I answered "yes." He went on to explain that they had bow sets with all the necessary equipment on sale for $34.95. I could buy a complete set for only $4.95 more than I could rent one. He explained that is why they had discontinued renting them. Did I think that was reasonable? My "yes" response led to a purchase of the set, and when I picked it up I purchased several more items at this shop and have since become a regular customer.'

THE SOCRATIC METHOD

Socrates, 'the gadfly of Athens', was one of the greatest philosophers the world has ever known. He did something that only a handful of men in all history have been able to do: he sharply changed the whole course of human thought; and now, twenty-four centuries after his death, he is honoured as one of the wisest persuaders who ever influenced this wrangling world.

His method? Did he tell people they were wrong? Oh, no, not Socrates. He was far too adroit for that. His whole technique, now called the 'Socratic method', was based upon getting a 'yes, yes' response. He asked questions with which his opponent would have to agree. He kept on winning one admission after another until he had an armful of yeses. He kept on asking questions until finally, almost without realising it, his opponents found themselves embracing a conclusion they would have bitterly denied a few minutes previously.

The next time we are tempted to tell someone he or she is wrong, let's remember old Socrates and ask a gentle question—a question that will get the 'yes, yes' response.

The Chinese have a proverb pregnant with the age-old wisdom of the Orient: 'He who treads softly goes far.'

POINTS TO REMEMBER:

1. If you want people to agree to something, keep on emphasising.
2. The yes-response technique.
3. Ask questions with only affirmative answers.

7

LISTENING TO LEARN

There are two very good reasons to listen to other people. You learn things that way, and people respond to those who listen to them.

This point sounds so obvious it looks almost silly sitting there in cold, hard type. But it's a lesson that most of us spend most of our lives forgetting to apply.

Hugh Downs was lucky. The longtime host of ABC's *20/20* program found out about listening early in his broadcasting career. This was back in the days of radio, when Downs was just getting started as an on-air interviewer. He witnessed first-hand how a simple failure to listen could trip up one of his most experienced colleagues.

'He was interviewing a man who had escaped from a Kremlin prison in the thirties,' Downs recalled. 'This guest was telling him how, for months, the prisoners had been trying to tunnel their way out of there. They'd dug and dug. They'd eaten the dirt. They'd arranged to have a saw smuggled in. And when they figured their tunnel was outside the prison walls, they began digging up. It was quite a dramatic story.

'Then this one midnight, they were finally ready to break loose. They had already sawed through a wooden platform above their heads. But when this one prisoner stuck his head out, he was shocked by what he saw. "When I got up," he told the interviewer, "I realized I was right in the middle of Josef Stalin's office."

"'And do you know what this interviewer said next?" Downs asked, recalling that long-ago day. "Do you have any hobbies?"

Not 'Are you serious? Josef Stalin's office?' Or 'Stalin wasn't working late that night, I hope.' Or 'So tell me, were you tempted to plop down in the butcher's chair and light up one of his cigars?' Had the interviewer been listening at all, he would have known to ask any number of follow-up questions the members of his audience undoubtedly had on their minds. But the interviewer's attention was off somewhere else. All he could manage was that ridiculous non sequitur. And his listeners were deprived of the climax to a fascinating tale.

'That's a true story,' Downs said. 'And I've heard other interviews like that, where the interviewer just didn't listen. It's amazing what people can miss. It's a part of the business I call the yeah-well interview.'

The importance of listening doesn't apply just to professional interviewers, of course. It is vital for anyone, anywhere, anytime, who hopes to communicate with others.

Listening is the single most important of all the communication skills. More important than stirring oratory. More important than a powerful voice. More important than the ability to speak multiple languages. More important even than a flair for the written word.

Good listening is truly where effective communication begins. It's surprising how few people really listen well, but successful leaders, more often than not, are the ones who have learned the value of listening.

'I don't sit on top of a mountain and get these visions of what we ought to do,' says Richard C. Buetow, director of quality at Motorola, Inc. 'I have to find out from other people. I have to do a lot of listening.'

Even a great communicator like Buetow, who is expected to articulate and communicate the Motorola vision just about everywhere he goes, must also know when not to talk. In his words, 'You have to be able to turn off your transmitter and listen—put the receiver on, let other people articulate ideas and nurture them.'

This understanding is a central part of Buetow's self-image as a business leader. He never talks about himself, for instance, as a grand strategist or a sophisticated corporate sage. He compares himself instead to a carrier pigeon.

'I don't solve one quality problem at Motorola,' he explains. 'If you ask me to do hardware, first thing I'll do is give you the telephone number of the person who is responsible for hardware. What I do is take the good ideas that I hear and carry them from place to place.'

The underlying truth here is self-evident: *no one can possibly know everything. Listening to others is the single best way to learn.*

This means listening to employees, to customers and to your friends and family—even to what harshest critics have to say. It doesn't mean becoming a captive of other people's opinions, but it does mean hearing them out.

You'll be thankful for many of their ideas.

Giorgio Maschietto, managing director of Lever Chile, S.A., the packaged-goods company, was responsible for running a string of factories in South America, including a giant Pepsodent toothpaste plant. The factory's production schedule was constantly being interrupted by the need to wash out the steel toothpaste tanks. One day one of the line operators made a suggestion, and Maschietto had the good sense to follow through.

'We were using just one tank,' he recalls. 'This line employee suggested we should put in a second tank. Now we can wash the first tank while using the second one, so there's no need to stop production anymore for tank washing. By adding a bolt in one case and by adding a small tank in another case, we've reduced changeover time by 70 per cent and significantly increased productivity.'

From the same source—the factory floor—Maschietto got a second toothpaste-production idea that was just as important. For years the factory had used a set of highly delicate and highly expensive scales beneath the toothpaste conveyer belt. Their purpose was to make sure each carton of toothpaste actually contained a tube. But the high-tech scales never quite worked. 'Sometimes,' Maschietto says, 'we used to seal up empty cartons and send them out.

'One of the ideas of the men on the line was to replace all this expensive machinery and just put a small jet of air across the conveyer belt where the tubes rolled by. The compressed air is regulated so that when the carton is empty, the pressure of the air is enough to throw the empty cartons off the belt.'

Many people think of listening as passive, talking as active. Even the clichés people use in conversation—'sit back and listen'—hint at this pervasive misunderstanding of what true listening is about. Simply hearing what someone says is a relatively passive activity. But engaged, effective listening is a highly active sport.

Andrés Navarro, president of SONDA, S.A., a South American computer-systems company, uses his native Spanish language to illustrate the difference between the two. 'In Spanish,' Navarro explains, ;we have two words, *oir* and *escuchar*,' the rough equivalent of 'to hear' and 'to listen'. To really listen is much more than just hearing. Many people, when they are hearing someone, they are really thinking to themselves, "What will I answer?" instead of trying to listen to what the person is saying.'

Active listening requires an intense involvement in a conversation, even when the listener's lips are still. That isn't always easy. It takes concentration. It requires genuine engagement. It calls for questioning and prodding. And it demands some kind of response, quick, thoughtful, on target and concise.

There are many ways of displaying active involvement in a conversation, ways that don't entail jumping in and interrupting the other person every seven words. The trick isn't to master every one of these techniques. Good listeners learn a few that they find comfortable and natural—and remember to put these few to work.

It can be an occasional nod, or an 'uh-huh', or an 'I see'. Some people like to shift their postures or lean forward in the chair. At appropriate moments, others smile or shake their heads. Strong eye contact is another way of indicating to your conversation-mate, 'Yes, I am listening closely to what you are telling me.'

And when the other person comes to a break in his or her talking, go ahead and ask a question that follows closely from what was just said.

What's important here isn't the precise listening technique that is chosen. None of these methods should ever be used in a wooden or rote way. These are just a few approaches that are worth being mindful of when the moment feels right. They will make the other person happier about speaking with you.

TEST TO EXAMINE IF YOU ARE AN ACTIVE LISTENER OR NOT

Elmer Wheeler was driving at much the same idea two generations ago when he wrote in his seminal book on salesmanship, *Sell the Sizzle Not the Steak*, 'A good listener bends toward you physically. He leans on you mentally with every word that you utter. He is "with you" every moment, nodding and smiling at the right times. He listens "a little closer". This isn't good advice just for salesmen,' Wheeler wrote. 'It is a sound rule to follow for social and business success.'

'A person who's actively listening,' says Bill Makahilahila, Director of Human Resources at SGS-Thomson Microelectronics, Inc., 'is usually the one who is asking questions and then waiting for a response, as opposed to coming up with an instant solution. Active listening is occurring when the employee feels and knows beyond a shadow of a doubt that you're not just jumping to conclusions.'

Makahilahila thinks this is such an important concept that he has even created an Active Listening Award for SGS-Thomson supervisors who excel at listening. He has come up with a three-question test for determining whether someone is listening actively or not:

1. Do you ask questions and wait for an answer?
2. Do you respond quickly and directly to the questions that are asked?
3. Does the other person *feel* you are listening actively to him or her?

A good listening environment—that's where listening begins. It's impossible to ever listen effectively when fear, anxiety or nervousness is present. That's why good teachers always make sure their classrooms are comfortable, hospitable places.

'I know for myself that when I'm nervous about something, I don't listen as well,' says kindergarten teacher Barbara Hammerman. 'I'm concerned with my own being. If the children are tense and nervous in a classroom, they're not free to listen.'

William Savel, retired chairman of Baskin-Robbins, the worldwide ice-cream and yogurt retailer, was once sent to Japan by the Nestlé Company to run marketing and sales.

'The first thing I did was to visit with a number of U.S. companies that had Japanese subsidiaries,' he recalls. He learned to speak Japanese. He slept in Japanese hotels. He ate Japanese food. He did everything he could think of to surround himself with things Japanese.

'The important thing is to listen,' Savel said, 'to really listen before you go in and start shooting your mouth off and telling everybody how smart you are. You've got to learn how dumb you are first. You have to go in and get to know the people, interact with them, don't put yourself above anyone else. Get around, talk to everybody, listen very intently and don't make up your mind too fast.'

Simply put, *People everywhere love to be listened to, and they almost always respond to others who listen to them.* Listening is one of the best techniques we have for showing respect to someone else. It's an indication that we consider them important human beings. It's our way of saying, 'What you think and do and believe is important to me.'

Strangely enough, listening to someone else's opinions is often the best method of getting them around to your way of thinking. Dean Rusk, President Johnson's secretary of state, knew this from decades of negotiating with some of the world's most stubborn political leaders. 'Listening is the way to persuade others with your ears.' It's true; listening can be a tremendously powerful tool for convincing others to see the world the way that you do.

'The real key,' says merchant banker Tom Saunders, of Saunders Karp & Company, 'is getting to understand a person and what he values and how he wants to look at investments and whether or not you could honestly say our approach was right and compatible for him.'

Saunders is in the business of advising big corporations about how to invest prodigious sums of money. His number-one technique? Listening to them. It all 'goes back to listening,' he says. 'What was really on his mind? Why had he said no? What was the real reason behind it?

'I've had a twenty-five-year relationship with AT&T, which has just been extraordinary. I think it's all basically been due to listening.'

Saunders goes on, 'I can give you the best-looking brochure. I can throw up all these slides. But still I've got to find out what's in there that's interesting to that person. What's on this person's mind? What does he think about? How does he look at things?'

The first step to becoming a strong, active listener is understanding how important good listening is. The second step is wanting to learn. Finally, you have to practice those budding listening skills.

'I learned mine in not such a pleasant way,' recalls Wolfgang R. Schmitt, CEO of Rubbermaid, Incorporated, the home-products giant. 'I learned mine by going through a divorce when I was young. I was very career-centred. In the process of trying to avoid the divorce, we went to a counsellor. That was really the first time I understood how crucial good listening is. Here was something that was important to me—my marriage—

and I wanted to try to retrieve it. That was the first time that somebody said to me some very straightforward things.'

About listening? 'Not just listening,' Schmitt says, 'but internalizing other people's feelings and thinking about them. Then being able to mirror them back, so you can demonstrate their importance to you.'

At Motorola small teams of employees are always encouraged to come in with their ideas. And the company's top executives sit quietly and listen. 'I've sat and listened to hundreds of teams tell me about all these issues and solutions and so on,' says Motorola's Richard Buetow. And it is out of those hundreds of conversations that Motorola's future has been built.

Those kinds of small group-discussions—hosted by executives who mostly keep their mouths shut—are a tremendously valuable way to institutionalize corporate listening. At Analog Devices, Chairman Ray Stata has created a technique he calls the CNA Roundtable. Meetings are held regularly. Small groups of employees from throughout the company are invited to sit down for no-holds-barred discussions with Stata and other top Analog executives. The general theme is 'creating a new Analog for the '90s', or CNA, the company's internal slogan these days.

'It's not just a matter of answering the questions people ask,' Stata explains. 'What I do after a certain amount of discussion is I'll say, "Now what I'd like to do is go around the table and have each individual tell me what their particular concerns are right now. What are your suggestions? Where are you coming from?" And I sit there and take copious notes.

'That's called listening,' he says. 'Afterwards, I write a memo that summarizes what I heard.'

Joe Booker took a new job as the leader of a quality-improvement program at the Allegheny Ludlum Corporation, an import-export company in the steel business. Quickly his enthusiasm turned to fear. 'The program had been in existence at the company's largest plant for about eighteen months, with poor acceptance by the plant's nearly two thousand employees. Since participation was voluntary, how would I get the departments to realize the need for quality improvement? In many cases they were already successful in using their own techniques.'

After some thought, Booker realized that what he needed to do was convince the employees that he was a competent team player who would be an asset to them. What this meant, he realized, was some hardcore listening.

'I began to visit each one of the plant's six departments with the goal of understanding how individuals felt about their products' quality,' he says. 'I avoided arguments about the program and guided each conversation to hear how that individual was key to the progress of quality improvement. I was able to find allies in each of the departments and with their aid encourage others to get involved in the challenge to meet world-class quality.

'Today our plant has the highest union-represented involvement in any of the company's finishing facilities. People understand how the next operation or department is their customer. This is a direct result of good listening and communication among all employees.'

David Luther at Corning has discovered exactly that same rule. 'One of the first questions I ask when I look at a communication plan is, "How long does it take before you see the word *listen*?" Most of these plans are full of "Let me tell you this" or "Let me tell you that and the other thing".'

At Corning, Luther developed a process for turning listening into a practical improvement tool. He explains how that process works. 'We'll call over to a factory. I want two groups of fifteen people, and I want them for five hours. And we'll come in. Usually there's the union head, he has an assistant, and I have an assistant. One of the union people and I will take one group of fifteen. My assistant and the other union person will take the other fifteen. So we have two people in front of each group.

'We take them through a process. The first thing we say is, "What's right about quality? Remember what it used to be like here ten years ago. Can you think about how quality is better now? Okay, let's put that on the wall."

'Second part: "What isn't right about quality? The only thing you can't complain about is your boss. Everything else is fair." And we put that on the wall.

'Then we'll take that second list and condense it to ten or twelve issues. There's always a little overlap. We want to get rid of the overlap. "Now we're going to vote. We've got twelve items here. You've each got three votes, and as I point to each of these twelve items here, if that's one of your more important quality issues, raise your hand."

'As you go through the list of twelve, six don't get any votes at all, a couple will get a few votes and maybe two will go right off the chart. So let's talk about those complaints.

'Then you take the two groups. You put them back together. You bring in the plant management. You have a spokesperson for each group get up and say, "Here's what my group said." So the first group says, "We don't understand what the plant manager thinks." And the second group gets up and says, "The plant manager never communicates to us." Even the dimmest plant manager will understand that he or she has got a major issue there and it's transparent. You can see the whole thing. It develops right there with his or her people.

'And there is no sending away questionnaires and rating them or coming back. I mean it's happened right before your eyes and you saw the coincidence. You know each of these teams did not know what the other team was saying. Now, we've done this maybe fifty times.'

These are all wonderful techniques. Many others have been developed inside well-led companies. Remember, the same two basic principles underlie them all:

1. Listening is still the best way to learn.
2. People respond to those who will listen to them.

The simple truth of the matter is that people love being listened to. It's true in the business world. It's true at home. It's true of just about everyone we come across in life.

The secret of influencing people lies not so much in being a good talker as in being a good listener. Most people trying to win others to their way of thinking do too much talking themselves. Let the other people talk themselves out. They know more about their business or problems than you do. So ask them questions. Let them tell you a few things.

If you disagree with them, you may be tempted to interrupt. But don't. It's dangerous. They won't pay attention to you while they still have a lot of ideas of theirs crying for expression. So listen patiently and with an open mind. Be sincere about it. Encourage them to express their ideas fully.

They will never forget. And you will learn a thing or two.

POINTS TO REMEMBER:

1. Effective communication begins with good listening.
2. Everyone wants to be heard.
3. You can influence people to go along with your ideas by conversing with them.

8

RESPECTING THE DIGNITY OF OTHERS

The world today is not just an old boys' club. It is a vastly more integrated, more diverse place than it was even a generation ago. Nowhere is that diversity more apparent than in the business world. Women, people from the LGBTQ+ community, people with disabilities, people from a wide array of racial and ethnic backgrounds—they're all a part of the equation today.

To succeed in that changed environment, it is absolutely essential to get along comfortably with everyone, whatever their background or culture may be. 'Only 15 or 20 per cent of the people entering the work force in the twenty-first century are not going to be minorities, women or immigrants,' predicts James Houghton, chairman of Corning, Incorporated. 'I mean, we're there. So unless you want to avail yourself of only 15 per cent of the talent out there, you'd better get diverse real quick.'

The best way to begin respecting another culture—or anything else, for that matter—is to learn about it. That was one of the main things that drew the late Arthur Ashe to professional tennis. 'I knew there was a lot of travel involved,' he said. 'That is really what I looked forward to. I wanted to go to those places. I wanted to see those things I'd only read about in the pages of *National Geographic*. I welcomed the opportunity to get to know them.

'Looking back on it now,' Ashe said in an interview just before his death, 'I rank that as one of my greatest sustained sets of recollections, the interactions I've had with a very wide variety of people from a lot of different cultures.

'You can look at traveling two ways,' Ashe said. 'You can have a very haughty attitude about your own culture. You go to other places and look condescendingly down at people who have come from civilizations many thousands of years older than yours. Maybe they're not as technologically advanced, and you think our system is better. The other way to look at it is to say, "Yes, their physical condition and circumstances are not good. But boy, what a rich theological or a rich cultural heritage they have. They've been here ten thousand years, so they must know something. We've only been around two hundred years." I much prefer the second approach.'

Even nations that are next-door neighbours often view each other differently. These differences must be recognized, respected and never condescended to. That's what Helmut Krings discovered moving back and forth between Germany and Switzerland. Krings, a German, is vice president for Central Europe at Sun Microsystems, a leading work-station manufacturer.

'I avoid comparisons,' he says. 'I try to avoid making any reference to Germany. What people hate most is if you are constantly saying what you do at home is right and suggesting that they're not doing things properly in their country.'

All people want respect for their own culture and language. It's only natural. Melchior Wathelet, the deputy prime minister of Belgium, grew up in a French-speaking Belgian family. Early in his political career, Wathelet decided to bridge his nation's language gap by learning to speak Flemish, the other official language. This made him Belgium's first French-Belgian politician to become fluent in both national languages. He showed his respect for all the nation's people. He became a national symbol of unity, and his political career soared. He had learned to live with diversity.

So how do you live comfortably with diversity in the corporate boardroom, in the university, in the local sales office, in the nonprofit organization, in the government today? The first step is a basic one: *put yourself in the other person's place.* Other people are living, breathing human beings just like you are. They have pressures at home. They want to succeed. They want to be treated with the same dignity, respect and understanding that you do.

'What's important,' says Thomas A. Doherty, the chairman of Fleet Bank, 'is the way in which people are treated on a daily basis. People want to be treated and recognized as individuals. That was true when I first came into banking thirty years ago, and I think one hundred years from now it's still going to be true' And Doherty is clear about the reason, 'Because we're all human beings.'

'What matters,' says Doherty, 'is treating people with respect. Small things like "Good morning" and "Thank you". My own feeling is that it's the role of management to create an atmosphere where people can perform at their highest level.' That atmosphere exists where people feel they're being respected and treated like individuals. It's absent where people feel they're just a number.

Most successful people have learned over the years that making others feel important is seldom accomplished by a single or even a few grand gestures. It's a process made up of many little touches.

Adriana Bitter at Scalamandré Silks has seen the power of

this reality. Times were tough for the fabric industry in the late 1980s and early 1990s, but the company survived by pulling together with the employees. 'Our people have been incredibly wonderful, working with us to get through this,' explains Bitter. 'I mean they've been fantastic. And I think it comes back to closeness. If we didn't have this closeness, why should they give anything back to us? You know you have to give to someone if you're going to get back. Anyway, that's our philosophy.'

How do you create that closeness? By showing respect and compassion and dignity to the people who work with you, by acknowledging that they're human beings who exist outside the work environment. At Bitter's company, that meant having the second-in-command gently correct a visiting speaker when he referred to the employees as mill workers instead of artisans. It meant Bitter's walking through the mill and talking to one of the designers about overcoming his fear of flying so he could take a planned vacation. It meant leaving the door to the president's office open and welcoming a bare-chested artisan when he needed to talk about problems in the dye house. It meant learning to speak Spanish to communicate better with the crew.

I used to tell the story of Jim Farley, Franklin Delano Roosevelt's campaign manager. Farley made it his business to remember—and use—the names of everyone he came into contact with. Often this meant remembering literally thousands of names. While running Roosevelt's re-election campaign, Farley would travel by boat, train and automobile, hopping from town to town, meeting hundreds of people at each stop. When he returned home after weeks on the road, he was exhausted. But he didn't rest before he had completed one task he considered absolutely essential: he'd send a personally signed letter to all the people he'd met on the campaign trail. And he'd start each letter with the person's first name: Dear Bill or Dear Rita.

Do people today still respond to those small things? You bet they do. Returning a phone call, remembering a name, treating someone respectfully—those are just about the most important things any leader can do. These basics, says ad man Burt Manning, 'are what works. That's how people separate themselves from the crowd, from the masses, by doing these basic things and never stopping.'

On a recent trip to Manning's office, a visitor was struck by a small gesture. There was only one hanger in the office. Manning took the visitor's coat and hung it on the hanger. He tossed his own coat over a doorknob. Trivial? Maybe, but don't think it wasn't noticed. Those are the little touches that send a message, 'I care about you. Your concerns are my concerns. We are in this together.' A real positive environment can be created that way.

And there is no better way of reinforcing it than by following the first step to the Golden Rule: *treat employees like colleagues, and don't condescend, dictate or berate.* They are your co-workers, after all, not your servants or your best friends. So treat them accordingly. Recognize the humanity that everyone in the organization shares. Playing the big boss doesn't motivate people to do anything but resent the individual who's pulling rank.

COMFORTABLE PEOPLE ARE MORE PRODUCTIVE

Given the great power of respect, why do so many managers fall into the habit of demeaning and yelling at the people who work for them? Often the reason is low self-esteem. 'Managers are exposed,' says John B. Robinson, Jr., executive vice president of Fleet Financial Group Inc., Fleet Bank's parent. 'They're on the line. I've often seen people—because it's a difficult situation—adopt an unnatural style. I'm thinking of some people I've seen over the years who tried to be tough managers and yet they aren't really tough managers. It's a cover maybe because of their own discomfort.'

Does it work? Almost never. 'They tend to abuse people verbally and try to demand respect by ordering people around or by being arbitrary or that sort of thing,' Robinson explains, 'and that's usually exactly counterproductive.' The reason is simple: people rarely respond well to intimidation.

It's much more effective to let your employees see that you are a human being too. Treat people like equals, like valuable assets, not like another piece of the company's machinery. 'What has to be done,' says Bill Makahilahila of SGS-Thomson Microelectronics, Inc., 'is to strip ourselves from position, strip ourselves from title in terms of how we viewed it in the past. View it as everyone contributing.'

For some business leaders this means a whole new understanding of the relationship between employee and boss. The right tone must be set for respect and open communication to occur. John Robinson believes, 'I guess one of the things that you need to do is maintain a sense of humility. It's so easy in the corporate world, the higher we get, to really believe that we're as important as our title suggests or that we're as smart as our position says.' Years ago, Robinson found a great way to remind himself that, despite the fancy titles he has had, he's just like everyone else he works with. 'I was the president of a bank when I was in my early thirties, and I'd feel very important about that,' he recalls. 'Then I'd come home and the baby would be wet and miserable, and I'd be changing the baby's diaper. Immediately it brought me back and gave me perspective. My kids are really what kept me in balance.'

Put yourself in the other person's place. Don't condescend. Those are both important. The second step to the Golden Rule:

engage people. Challenge them. Invite their input. Encourage their cooperation.

Work, in most cases, is as big a part of their lives as it is of yours. Almost certainly they want to be involved. They want to be engaged. They want to be challenged and stretched. They don't want their opinions ignored.

People who are passionate and involved with what they do will do it well. As Ray Stata of Analog Devices Inc., puts it, 'What people want is a feeling of importance, a feeling of impact, a feeling of influence.'

How can this feeling be created? By empowering your employees, challenging them, involving them in the planning of your organization. Says Stata, 'I think that the most important thing is that people have job assignments and tasks to do that they feel are commensurate with their ability or maybe stretch them somewhat beyond their ability. I think the most important part of motivation is to try to link the task to the individual in such a way that it is a real challenge, that there is a stretch of expectation.'

Rubbermaid figured this out early. That company radically pioneered the employee empowerment method of management. When Rubbermaid had to design a multimillion-dollar piece of new equipment in the late 1980s, the bosses didn't rule the day. Instead, Rubbermaid had the employees, the people who actually would be using the machine, lead the process. Wolfgang Schmitt explains, 'We put together a team of six people. These were all production associates with one management associate. They went out to the various companies who make these kinds of equipment and did the benchmarking. They were the ones who made the recommendation on what to buy. They were the ones who went over and trained in Europe, in this case in Germany, on the machines. They came back with the supplier's people and set it up. They managed it. They scheduled it. They ensured the quality of it. They did the preventive maintenance.'

The results of this approach for Rubbermaid have been profound. The company has one of the highest employee-retention rates in the business, and Rubbermaid employees work. From 1982 to 1992 Rubbermaid paid an average annual rate of return to investors of 25.7 per cent.

Bill Makahilahila describes the process of empowering his employees as one of his most important roles. It's often a difficult one. It involves instilling a sense of confidence in employees, 'helping employees process their own thoughts and their own ideas and then solidifying that in their minds so they can feel self-confident in carrying out and executing their skills,' as Makahilahila puts it. It involves hanging back, supporting the decisions, not taking over.

'In my mind there is no such thing as a right or wrong decision,' he says. 'I need to give you the full authority to make the decision. Now, if it's not the best decision that has been made, we'll discuss it. But if it is the best decision, I'll reinforce it to you and help you recognize it.'

It's difficult, but the results justify the effort. Employees become committed to what they're doing. Perhaps Ray Stata says it best, 'I think the pinnacle of what's important, particularly for educated, professional, knowledgeable workers, is the whole issue of self-actualization, self-fulfilment. So the notion of continuing improvement and growth in the development of their capabilities is at the end of the day the most important thing to motivate people.'

Treat people well, treat them like equals and engage them in the team process of work. There is one final way to create the workplace of dignity: *humanize the organization in ways big and small.*

Symbolic efforts can play a big role here. For instance, get out from behind that big executive desk. Joyce Harvey of Harmon Associates Corporation has a small conference table in her office, and she uses it. 'We sit around and talk,' Harvey says. 'I very often have a midday meeting, and I always make it a habit to bring lunch for any employee who's staying through the lunch hour. It makes it more casual and more informal, and it shows that we care and respect their time.'

E. Martin Gibson, chairman of Corning Lab Services Inc., moves beyond symbolism. He thinks that humanizing an organization is so important that he's even structured the physical plants of his facilities with that in mind. 'I think employees working in a single location with ten, fifteen, twenty thousand people is a disaster,' says Gibson. 'I mean I can't imagine myself getting out of the car and walking through a parking lot with ten thousand people in a huge complex. I would always ask myself the question, "If I vaporized, would anyone even know it?"

'Chances are, no. Or all they would say is, "Where's old what's-his-name?"'

A worker who feels this disassociated isn't going to be very committed to an organization. Corning Lab Services, knowing this, has come up with a solution. The company has thirty-two different physical locations. While one of them is large—1,900 employees—the rest range between three hundred and six hundred employees.

The results? 'We've got people who, when they go to work every morning, know each other's names,' said Gibson. 'If they vaporized, someone would know. You know people would miss you because you're working in a small unit. Everyone knows your first name. It's exciting.'

Wolfgang Schmitt of Rubbermaid agrees. That's why he

tries to keep his facilities in the four-to-six-hundred-employee range. Why that size? To save money? Not really. 'What we think is really crucial is the people relationships,' explains Schmitt. 'When you get beyond the four- to six-hundred number, we think the personalized aspect of that relationship, the understanding, the empathy goes away. You start having to layer in overhead to artificially create understanding rather than having it sort of organically present. So both from a humanistic viewpoint and from a pure cost viewpoint, it's just as prudent, really smart, to stay in these units that are about that size.'

Schmitt reached that conclusion when interviews with employees revealed that that size pleased the employees. 'We find that the more we stick with that mode, the more people feel good about being a part of the organization, the more connectedness there is.'

These issues are vitally important, and they aren't just for top managers. All of us—at whatever position—will go further and accomplish more by respecting the importance and the dignity of others, whatever their position, background or relationship to us.

This is not a new concept. Years ago, I was applying it to people all over the world. 'Do you feel that you are superior to the Japanese?' I asked. 'The truth is that the Japanese consider themselves far superior to you. Do you consider yourselves superior to the Hindus in India? That is your privilege. But a million Hindus feel infinitely superior to you.

'Each nation feels superior to other nations. That breeds patriotism and wars.

'The unvarnished truth is that almost all the people you meet feel superior to you in some way. And a sure way to their hearts is let them realize in some subtle way that you recognize their importance in the world and recognize it sincerely.'

POINTS TO REMEMBER:

1. You have to change with the changing environment and culture.
2. Avoid making comparisons.
3. Put yourself in the other person's place.

9

DON'T TRY TO SAW SAWDUST

As I write this sentence, I can look out of my window and see some dinosaur tracks in my garden—dinosaur tracks embedded in shale and stone. I purchased those dinosaur tracks from the Peabody Museum of Yale University; and I have a letter from the curator of the Peabody Museum, saying that those tracks were made 180 million years ago. Even a Mongolian idiot wouldn't dream of trying to go back 180 million years to change those tracks. Yet that would not be any more foolish than worrying because we can't go back and change what happened 180 seconds ago—and a lot of us are doing just that. To be sure, we may do something to *modify the effects* of what happened 180 seconds ago; but we can't possibly change the event that occurred then.

There is only one way on God's green footstool that the past can be constructive; and that is by calmly analysing our past mistakes and profiting by them—and forgetting them.

I know that is true; but have I always had the courage and sense to do it? To answer that question, let me tell you about a fantastic experience I had years ago. I let more than three hundred thousand dollars slip through my fingers without making a penny's profit. It happened like this—I launched a large-scale enterprise in adult education, opened branches in various cities and spent money lavishly in overhead and advertising. I was so busy with teaching that I had neither the time nor the desire to look after finances. I was too naïve to realize that I needed an astute business manager to watch expenses.

Finally, after about a year, I discovered a sobering and shocking truth. I discovered that in spite of our enormous intake, we had not netted any profit whatever. After discovering that, I should have done two things. First, I should have had the sense to do what George Washington Carver, the agricultural scientist, did when he lost forty thousand dollars in a bank crash—the savings of a lifetime. When someone asked him if he knew he was bankrupt, he replied, 'Yes, I heard,'—and went on with his teaching. He wiped the loss out of his mind so completely that he never mentioned it again.

Here is the second thing I should have done—I should have analysed my mistakes and learned a lasting lesson.

But frankly, I didn't do either one of these things. Instead, I went into a tailspin of worry. For months I was in a daze. I lost sleep and I lost weight. Instead of learning a lesson from this enormous mistake, I went right ahead and did the same thing again on a smaller scale!

It is embarrassing for me to admit all this stupidity; but I discovered long ago that 'it is easier to teach twenty what were good to be done than to be one of the twenty to follow mine own teaching.'

How I wish that I had had the privilege of attending the George Washington High School here in New York and studying under Mr Brandwine—the same teacher who taught Allen Saunders, of 939 Woodycrest Avenue, Bronx, New York!

Mr Saunders told me that the teacher of his hygiene class, Mr Brandwine, taught him one of the most valuable lessons he had ever learned. 'I was only in my teens,' said Allen Saunders as he told me the story, 'but I was a worrier even then. I used to stew and fret about the mistakes I had made. If I turned in an examination paper, I used to lie awake and chew my fingernails for fear I hadn't passed. I was always living over the things I had done, and wishing I'd done them differently; thinking over the things I had said, and wishing I'd said them better.

'Then one morning, our class filed into the science laboratory, and there was the teacher, Mr Brandwine, with a bottle of milk prominently displayed on the edge of the desk. We all sat down, staring at the milk and wondering what it had to do with the hygiene course he was teaching. Then, all of a sudden, Mr Brandwine stood up, swept the bottle of milk with a crash into the sink—and shouted, "Don't cry over spilt milk!"

'He then made us all come to the sink and look at the wreckage. "Take a good look," he told us, "because I want you to remember this lesson the rest of your lives. That milk is gone—you can see it's down the drain; and all the fussing and hair-pulling in the world won't bring back a drop of it. With a little thought and prevention, that milk might have been saved. But it's too late now—all we can do is write it off, forget it and go on to the next thing."

'"That one little demonstration," Allen Saunders told me, "stuck with me long after I'd forgotten my solid geometry and Latin. In fact, it taught me more about practical living than anything else in my four years of high school. It taught me to keep from spilling milk if I could; but to forget it completely, once it was spilled and had gone down the drain."'

Some readers are going to snort at the idea of making so much over a hackneyed proverb like 'Don't cry over spilt milk.' I know it is trite, commonplace and a platitude. I know we have heard it a thousand times. But I also know that these hackneyed proverbs contain the very essence of the distilled wisdom of all ages. They have come out of the fiery experience of the human race and have been handed down through countless generations. If we were to read everything that has ever been written about worry by the great scholars of all time, we would never read anything more basic or more profound than such hackneyed proverbs as 'Don't cross your bridges until you come to them' and 'Don't cry over spilt milk'. If we only applied those two proverbs—instead of snorting at them—we wouldn't need this book at all. In fact, if we applied most of the old proverbs, we would lead almost perfect lives. However, knowledge isn't power until it is applied; and the purpose of this book is not to tell you something new. The purpose of this book is to remind you of what you already know and to kick you in the shins and inspire you to do something about applying it.

HAVE YOU EVER SAWED SAWDUST?

I have always admired a man like the late Fred Fuller Shedd, who had a gift for stating an old truth in a new and picturesque way. He was editor of the *Philadelphia Bulletin;* and, while addressing a college graduating class, he asked, 'How many of you have ever sawed wood? Let's see your hands.' Most of them had. Then he enquired, 'How many of you have ever sawed *sawdust?*' No hands went up.

'Of course, you can't saw sawdust!' Mr Shedd exclaimed. 'It's already sawed! And it's the same with the past. When you start worrying about things that are over and done with, you're merely trying to saw sawdust.'

When Connie Mack, the grand old man of baseball, was eighty-one years old, I asked him if he had ever worried over games that were lost.

'Oh, yes, I used to,' Connie Mack told me. 'But I got over that foolishness long years ago. I found out it didn't get me anywhere at all. You can't grind any grain,' he said, 'with water that has already gone down the creek.'

No, you can't grind any grain—and you can't saw any logs with water that has already gone down the creek. But you can saw wrinkles in your face and ulcers in your stomach.

I had dinner with Jack Dempsey last Thanksgiving; and he told me over the turkey and cranberry sauce about the fight in which he lost the heavyweight championship to Tunney. Naturally, it was a blow to his ego. 'In the midst of that fight,' he told me, 'I suddenly realized I had become an old man... At the end of the tenth round, I was still on my feet, but that was about all. My face was puffed and cut, and my eyes were nearly closed... I saw the referee raise Gene Tunney's hand in token of victory... I was no longer champion of the world. I started back in the rain—back through the crowd to my dressing room. As I passed, some people tried to grab my hand. Others had tears in their eyes.

'A year later, I fought Tunney again. But it was no use. I was through forever. It was hard to keep from worrying about it all, but I said to myself, "I'm not going to live in the past or cry over spilt milk. I am going to take this blow on the chin and not let it floor me."'

And that is precisely what Jack Dempsey did. How? By saying to himself over and over, 'I won't worry about the past'? No, that would merely have forced him to think of his past worries. He did it by accepting and writing off his defeat and then concentrating on plans for the future. He did it by running the Jack Dempsey Restaurant on Broadway and the Great Northern Hotel on 57th Street. He did it by promoting prize fights and giving boxing exhibitions. He did it by getting so busy on something constructive that he had neither the time nor the temptation to worry about the past. 'I have had a better time during the last ten years,' Jack Dempsey said, 'than I had when I was champion.'

Mr Dempsey told me that he had not read many books; but, without knowing it, he was following Shakespeare's advice, 'Wise men ne'er sit and wail their loss, but cheerily seek how to redress their harms.'

As I read History and Biography and observe people under trying circumstances, I am constantly astonished and inspired by some people's ability to write off their worries and tragedies and go on living fairly happy lives.

I once paid a visit to Sing Sing, and the thing that astonished me most was that the prisoners there appeared to be about as happy as the average person on the outside. I commented on it to Lewis E. Lawes—then warden of Sing Sing—and he told me that when criminals first arrive at Sing Sing, they are likely to be resentful and bitter. But after a few months, the majority of the more intelligent ones write off their misfortunes and settle down and accept prison life calmly and make the best of it. Warden Lawes told me about one Sing Sing prisoner—a gardener—who *sang* as he cultivated the vegetables and flowers inside the prison walls.

That Sing Sing prisoner who sang as he cultivated the flowers showed a lot more sense than most of us do. He knew that:

The Moving Finger writes; and, having writ,
Moves on: nor all your Piety nor Wit Shall lure it back to cancel half a Line,
Nor all your Tears wash out a Word of it.

So why waste the tears? Of course, we have been guilty

of blunders and absurdities! And so what? Who hasn't? Even Napoleon lost one-third of all the important battles he had fought. Perhaps our batting average is no worse than Napoleon's. Who knows?

POINTS TO REMEMBER:

1. No matter what you can't change the outcome of what happened in the past.
2. Analyse and learn from your past mistakes.
3. Instead of whining about your failures, buckle up and work.

10

THE HIGH ROAD TO REASON

If your temper is aroused and you tell 'em a thing or two, you will have a fine time unloading your feelings. But what about the other person? Will he share your pleasure? Will your belligerent tones, your hostile attitude, make it easy for him to agree with you?

'If you come at me with your fists doubled,' said Woodrow Wilson, 'I think I can promise you that mine will double as fast as yours; but if you come to me and say, "Let us sit down and take counsel together, and, if we differ from each other, understand why it is that we differ, just what the points at issue are," we will presently find that we are not so far apart after all, that the points on which we differ are few and the points on which we agree are many, and that if we only have the patience and the candour and the desire to get together, we will get together.'

Nobody appreciated the truth of Woodrow Wilson's statement more than John D. Rockefeller, Jr. Back in 1915, Rockefeller was the most fiercely despised man in Colorado. One of the bloodiest strikes in the history of American industry had been shocking the state for two terrible years. Irate, belligerent miners were demanding higher wages from the Colorado Fuel and Iron Company; Rockefeller controlled that company. Property had been destroyed; troops had been called out. Blood had been shed. Strikers had been shot, their bodies riddled with bullets.

At a time like that, with the air seething with hatred, Rockefeller wanted to win the strikers to his way of thinking. And he did it. How? Here's the story. After weeks spent in making friends, Rockefeller addressed the representatives of the strikers. This speech, in its entirety, is a masterpiece. It produced astonishing results. It calmed the tempestuous waves of hate that threatened to engulf Rockefeller. It won him a host of admirers. It presented facts in such a friendly manner that the strikers went back to work without saying another word about the increase in wages for which they had fought so violently.

The opening of that remarkable speech follows. Note how it fairly glows with friendliness. Rockefeller, remember, was talking to men who, a few days previously, had wanted to hang him by the neck to a sour apple tree; yet he couldn't have been more gracious, more friendly if he had addressed a group of medical missionaries. His speech was radiant with such phrases as I am *proud* to be here, having *visited* in *your homes,* met many of your wives and children, we meet here not as strangers, but as *friends*...spirit of *mutual friendship,* our *common interests,* it is only by *your courtesy* that I am here.

'This is a red-letter day in my life,' Rockefeller began. 'It is the first time I have ever had the good fortune to meet the representatives of the employees of this great company, its officers and superintendents, together, and I can assure you that I am proud to be here, and that I shall remember this gathering as long as I live. Had this meeting been held two weeks ago, I should have stood here a stranger to most of you, recognizing a few faces. Having had the opportunity last week of visiting all the camps in the southern coal field and of talking individually with practically all of the representatives, except those who were away; having visited in your homes, met many of your wives and children, we meet here not as strangers, but as friends, and it is in that spirit of mutual friendship that I am glad to have this opportunity to discuss with you our common interests.

'Since this is a meeting of the officers of the company and the representatives of the employees, it is only by your courtesy that I am here, for I am not so fortunate as to be either one or the other; and yet I feel that I am intimately associated with you men, for, in a sense, I represent both the stockholders and the directors.'

Isn't that a superb example of the fine art of making friends out of enemies?

Suppose Rockefeller had taken a different tack. Suppose he had argued with these miners and hurled devastating facts in their faces. Suppose he had told them by his tone and insinuations that they were wrong. Suppose that, by all the rules of logic, he had proved that they were wrong. What would have happened? More anger would have been stirred up, more hatred, more revolt.

If a man's heart is rankling with discord and ill feeling toward you, you can't win him to your way of thinking with all the logic in Christendom. Scolding parents and domineering bosses and husbands and nagging wives ought to realize that people don't want to change their minds. They can't be forced or driven to agree with you or me. But they may possibly be led to, if we are gentle and friendly, ever so gentle and ever so friendly.

Lincoln said that, in effect, over a hundred years ago. Here are his words:

> *It is an old and true maxim that 'a drop of honey catches more flies than a gallon of gall.' So with men, if you would*

win a man to your cause, first convince him that you are his sincere friend. Therein is a drop of honey that catches his heart; which, say what you will, is the great high road to his reason.

Business executives have learned that it pays to be friendly to strikers. For example, when 2,500 employees in the White Motor Company's plant struck for higher wages and a union shop, Robert F. Black, then president of the company, didn't lose his temper and condemn and threaten and talk of tyranny and communists. He actually praised the strikers. He published an advertisement in the Cleveland papers, complimenting them on 'the peaceful way in which they laid down their tools.' Finding the strike pickets idle, he bought them a couple of dozen baseball bats and gloves and invited them to play ball on vacant lots. For those who preferred bowling, he rented a bowling alley.

This friendliness on Mr Black's part did what friendliness always does: it begot friendliness. So the strikers borrowed brooms, shovels and rubbish carts, and began picking up matches, papers, cigarette stubs and cigar butts around the factory. Imagine it! Imagine strikers tidying up the factory grounds while battling for higher wages and recognition of the union. Such an event had never been heard of before in the long, tempestuous history of American labour wars. That strike ended with a compromise settlement within a week—ended without any ill feeling or rancour.

The use of gentleness and friendliness is demonstrated day after day by people who have learned that a drop of honey catches more flies than a gallon of gall. F. Gale Connor of Lutherville, Maryland, proved this when he had to take his four-month-old car to the service department of the car dealer for the third time. He told our class, 'It was apparent that talking to, reasoning with or shouting at the service manager was not going to lead to a satisfactory resolution of my problems.

'I walked over to the showroom and asked to see the agency owner, Mr White. After a short wait, I was ushered into Mr White's office. I introduced myself and explained to him that I had bought my car from his dealership because of the recommendations of friends who had had previous dealings with him. I was told that his prices were very competitive and his service was outstanding. He smiled with satisfaction as he listened to me. I then explained the problem I was having with the service department. "I thought you might want to be aware of any situation that might tarnish your fine reputation," I added. He thanked me for calling this to his attention and assured me that my problem would be taken care of. Not only did he personally get involved, but he also lent me his car to use while mine was being repaired.'

Aesop was a Greek slave who lived at the court of Croesus and spun immortal fables six hundred years before Christ. Yet the truths he taught about human nature are just as true in Boston and Birmingham now as they were twenty-six centuries ago in Athens. The sun can make you take off your coat more quickly than the wind; and kindliness, the friendly approach, and appreciation can make people change their minds more readily than all the bluster and storming in the world.

Remember what Lincoln said, 'A drop of honey catches more flies than a gallon of gall.'

> **POINTS TO REMEMBER:**
>
> 1. If you only have the patience and the candour and the desire to get together with other people, you will get together.
> 2. Fine art of making friends out of enemies.
> 3. Logic or dominance won't ever get anyone on your side. Try being friendly instead.

11

THINK BEFORE YOU CRITICISE

You will find examples of the futility of criticism bristling on a thousand pages of history. Take, for example, the famous quarrel between Theodore Roosevelt and President Taft—a quarrel that split the Republican party, put Woodrow Wilson in the White House and wrote bold, luminous lines across the First World War and altered the flow of history. Let's review the facts quickly. When Theodore Roosevelt stepped out of the White House in 1908, he supported Taft, who was elected President. Then Theodore Roosevelt went off to Africa to shoot lions. When he returned, he exploded. He denounced Taft for his conservatism, tried to secure the nomination for a third term himself, formed the Bull Moose party and all but demolished the G.O.P. In the election that followed, William Howard Taft and the Republican party carried only two states—Vermont and Utah. The most disastrous defeat the party had ever known.

Theodore Roosevelt blamed Taft, but did President Taft blame himself? Of course not. With tears in his eyes, Taft said, 'I don't see how I could have done any differently from what I have.'

Who was to blame? Roosevelt or Taft? Frankly, I don't know and I don't care. The point I am trying to make is that all of Theodore Roosevelt's criticism didn't persuade Taft that he was wrong. It merely made Taft strive to justify himself and to reiterate with tears in his eyes, 'I don't see how I could have done any differently from what I have.'

Or, take the Teapot Dome oil scandal. It kept the newspapers ringing with indignation in the early 1920s. It rocked the nation! Within the memory of living men, nothing like it had ever happened before in American public life. Here are the bare facts of the scandal: Albert B. Fall, secretary of the interior in Harding's cabinet, was entrusted with the leasing of government oil reserves at Elk Hill and Teapot Dome—oil reserves that had been set aside for the future use of the Navy. Did Secretary Fall permit competitive bidding? No sir. He handed the fat, juicy contract outright to his friend Edward L. Doheny. And what did Doheny do? He gave Secretary Fall what he was pleased to call a 'loan' of $100,000. Then, in a high-handed manner, Secretary Fall ordered United States Marines into the district to drive off competitors whose adjacent wells were sapping oil out of the Elk Hill reserves. These competitors, driven off their ground at the ends of guns and bayonets, rushed into court— and blew the lid off the Teapot Dome scandal. A stench arose so vile that it ruined the Harding Administration, nauseated an entire nation, threatened to wreck the Republican party and put Albert B. Fall behind prison bars.

Fall was condemned viciously—condemned as few men in public life have ever been. Did he repent? Never! Years later Herbert Hoover intimated in a public speech that President Harding's death had been due to mental anxiety and worry because a friend had betrayed him. When Mrs Fall heard that, she sprang from her chair, she wept, she shook her fists at fate and screamed, 'What! Harding betrayed by Fall? No! My husband never betrayed anyone. This whole house full of gold would not tempt my husband to do wrong. He is the one who has been betrayed and led to the slaughter and crucified.'

There you are; human nature in action, wrongdoers, blaming everybody but themselves. We are all like that. So when you and I are tempted to criticise someone tomorrow, let's remember Al Capone, 'Two Gun' Crowley and Albert Fall. Let's realise that criticisms are like homing pigeons. They always return home. Let's realise that the person we are going to correct and condemn will probably justify himself or herself, and condemn us in return; or, like the gentle Taft, will say, 'I don't see how I could have done any differently from what I have.'

On the morning of 15 April 1865, Abraham Lincoln lay dying in a hall bedroom of a cheap lodging house directly across the street from Ford's Theatre, where John Wilkes Booth had shot him. Lincoln's long body lay stretched diagonally across a sagging bed that was too short for him. A cheap reproduction of Rosa Bonheur's famous painting *The Horse Fair* hung above the bed, and a dismal gas jet flickered yellow light.

As Lincoln lay dying, Secretary of War Stanton said, 'There lies the most perfect ruler of men that the world has ever seen.'

What was the secret of Lincoln's success in dealing with people? I studied the life of Abraham Lincoln for ten years and devoted all of three years to writing and rewriting a book entitled *Lincoln the Unknown*. I believe I have made as detailed and exhaustive study of Lincoln's personality and home life as it is possible for any being to make. I made a special study of Lincoln's method of dealing with people. Did he indulge in criticism? Oh, yes. As a young man in the Pigeon Creek Valley of Indiana, he not only criticised but he wrote letters and poems ridiculing people and dropped these letters on the country roads where they were sure to be found. One of these letters aroused resentments that burned for a lifetime.

Even after Lincoln had become a practising lawyer in

Springfield, Illinois, he attacked his opponents openly in letters published in the newspapers. But he did this just once too often.

In the autumn of 1842 he ridiculed a vain, pugnacious politician by the name of James Shields. Lincoln lampooned him through an anonymous letter published in the Springfield *Journal*. The town roared with laughter. Shields, sensitive and proud, boiled with indignation. He found out who wrote the letter, leapt on his horse, started after Lincoln and challenged him to fight a duel. Lincoln didn't want to fight. He was opposed to duelling, but he couldn't get out of it and save his honour. He was given the choice of weapons. Since he had very long arms, he chose cavalry broadswords and took lessons in sword fighting from a West Point graduate; and, on the appointed day, he and Shields met on a sandbar in the Mississippi River, prepared to fight to the death; but, at the last minute, their seconds interrupted and stopped the duel.

That was the most lurid personal incident in Lincoln's life. It taught him an invaluable lesson in the art of dealing with people. Never again did he write an insulting letter. Never again did he ridicule anyone. And from that time on, he almost never criticised anybody for anything.

Time after time, during the Civil War, Lincoln put a new general at the head of the Army of the Potomac, and each one in turn—McClellan, Pope, Burnside, Hooker, Meade—blundered tragically and drove Lincoln to pacing the floor in despair. Half the nation savagely condemned these incompetent generals, but Lincoln, 'with malice toward none, with charity for all,' held his peace. One of his favourite quotations was, 'Judge not, that ye be not judged.'

And when Mrs Lincoln and others spoke harshly of the southern people, Lincoln replied, 'Don't criticise them; they are just what we would be under similar circumstances.'

Yet if any man ever had occasion to criticise, surely it was Lincoln. Let's take just one illustration:

The Battle of Gettysburg was fought during the first three days of July 1863. During the night of 4 July, Lee began to retreat southward while storm clouds deluged the country with rain. When Lee reached the Potomac with his defeated army, he found a swollen, impassable river in front of him, and a victorious Union Army behind him. Lee was in a trap. He couldn't escape. Lincoln saw that. Here was a golden, heaven-sent opportunity—the opportunity to capture Lee's army and end the war immediately. So, with a surge of hope, Lincoln ordered Meade not to call a council of war but to attack Lee immediately. Lincoln telegraphed his orders and then sent a special messenger to Meade demanding immediate action.

And what did General Meade do? He did the very opposite of what he was told to do. He called a council of war in direct violation of Lincoln's orders. He hesitated. He procrastinated. He telegraphed all manner of excuses. He refused point-blank to attack Lee. Finally, the waters receded and Lee escaped over the Potomac with his forces.

Lincoln was furious. 'What does this mean?' Lincoln cried to his son Robert. 'Great God! What does this mean? We had them within our grasp, and had only to stretch forth our hands and they were ours; yet nothing that I could say or do could make the army move. Under the circumstances, almost any general could have defeated Lee. If I had gone up there, I could have whipped him myself.'

In bitter disappointment, Lincoln sat down and wrote Meade this letter. And remember, at this period of his life Lincoln was extremely conservative and restrained in his phraseology. So this letter coming from Lincoln in 1863 was tantamount to the severest rebuke.

> My dear General,
> *I do not believe you appreciate the magnitude of the misfortune involved in Lee's escape. He was within our easy grasp, and to have closed upon him would, in connection with our other late successes, have ended the war. As it is, the war will be prolonged indefinitely. If you could not safely attack Lee last Monday, how can you possibly do so south of the river, when you can take with you very few—no more than two-thirds of the force you then had in hand? It would be unreasonable to expect and I do not expect that you can now effect much. Your golden opportunity is gone, and I am distressed immeasurably because of it.*

What do you suppose Meade did when he read the letter?

Meade never saw that letter. Lincoln never mailed it. It was found among his papers after his death.

My guess is—and this is only a guess—that after writing that letter, Lincoln looked out of the window and said to himself, 'Just a minute. Maybe I ought not to be so hasty. It is easy enough for me to sit here in the quiet of the White House and order Meade to attack; but if I had been up at Gettysburg, and if I had seen as much blood as Meade has seen during the last week, and if my ears had been pierced with the screams and shrieks of the wounded and dying, maybe I wouldn't be so anxious to attack either. If I had Meade's timid temperament, perhaps I would have done just what he had done. Anyhow, it is water under the bridge now. If I send this letter, it will relieve my feelings, but it will make Meade try to justify himself. It will make him condemn me. It will arouse hard feelings, impair all his further usefulness as a commander and perhaps force him to resign from the army.'

So, as I have already said, Lincoln put the letter aside, for he had learnt by bitter experience that sharp criticisms and rebukes almost invariably end in futility.

FUTILITY OF CURT CRITICISM

Theodore Roosevelt said that when he, as President, was confronted with a perplexing problem, he used to lean back and look up at a large painting of Lincoln which hung above his desk in the White House and ask himself, 'What would Lincoln do if he were in my shoes? How would he solve this problem?'

Mark Twain lost his temper occasionally and wrote letters that turned the paper brown. For example, he once wrote to a man who had aroused his ire, 'The thing for you is a burial permit. You have only to speak and I will see that you get it.' On another occasion he wrote to an editor about a proofreader's attempts to 'improve my spelling and punctuation.' He ordered, 'Set the matter according to my copy hereafter and see that the proofreader retains his suggestions in the mush of his decayed brain.'

The writing of these stinging letters made Mark Twain feel better. They allowed him to blow off steam, and the letters didn't do any real harm, because Mark's wife secretly lifted them out of the mail. They were never sent.

Do you know someone you would like to change and regulate and improve? Good! That is fine. I am all in favour of it. But why not begin on yourself? From a purely selfish standpoint, that is a lot more profitable than trying to improve others—yes, and a lot less dangerous. 'Don't complain about the snow on your neighbour's roof,' said Confucious, 'when your own doorstep is unclean.'

When I was still young and trying to impress people, I

wrote a foolish letter to Richard Harding Davis, an author who once loomed large on the literary horizon of America. I was preparing a magazine article about authors, and I asked Davis to tell me about his method of work. A few weeks earlier, I had received a letter from someone with this notation at the bottom: 'Dictated but not read.' I was quite impressed. I felt that the writer must be very big and busy and important. I wasn't the slightest bit busy, but I was eager to make an impression on Richard Harding Davis, so I ended my short note with the words, 'Dictated but not read.'

He never troubled to answer the letter. He simply returned it to me with this scribbled across the bottom, 'Your bad manners are exceeded only by your bad manners.' True, I had blundered, and perhaps I deserved this rebuke. But, being human, I resented it. I resented it so sharply that when I read of the death of Richard Harding Davis ten years later, the one thought that still persisted in my mind—I am ashamed to admit—was the hurt he had given me.

If you and I want to stir up a resentment tomorrow that may rankle across the decades and endure until death, just let us indulge in a little stinging criticism—no matter how certain we are that it is justified.

When dealing with people, let us remember we are not dealing with creatures of logic. We are dealing with creatures of emotion, creatures bristling with prejudices and motivated by pride and vanity.

Bitter criticism caused the sensitive Thomas Hardy, one of the finest novelists ever to enrich English literature, to give up forever the writing of fiction. Criticism drove Thomas Chatterton, the English poet, to suicide.

Benjamin Franklin, tactless in his youth, became so diplomatic, so adroit at handling people, that he was made

American Ambassador to France. The secret of his success? 'I will speak ill of no man,' he said, '. . . and speak all the good I know of everybody.'

Any fool can criticise, condemn and complain—and most fools do.

But it takes character and self-control to be understanding and forgiving.

'A great man shows his greatness,' said Carlyle, 'by the way he treats little men.'

Bob Hoover, a famous test pilot and frequent performer at air shows, was returning to his home in Los Angeles from an air show in San Diego. As described in the magazine *Flight Operations*, at 300 feet in the air, both engines suddenly stopped. By deft manoeuvring he managed to land the plane, but it was badly damaged although nobody was hurt.

Hoover's first act after the emergency landing was to inspect the aeroplane's fuel. Just as he suspected, the World War II propeller plane he had been flying had been fuelled with jet fuel rather than gasoline.

Upon returning to the airport, he asked to see the mechanic who had serviced his aeroplane. The young man was sick with the agony of his mistake. Tears streamed down his face as Hoover approached. He had just caused the loss of a very expensive plane and could have caused the loss of three lives as well.

You can imagine Hoover's anger. One could anticipate the tongue-lashing that this proud and precise pilot would unleash for that carelessness. But Hoover didn't scold the mechanic; he didn't even criticise him. Instead, he put his big arm around the man's shoulder and said, 'To show you I'm sure that you'll never do this again, I want you to service my F-51 tomorrow.'

Often parents are tempted to criticise their children. You would expect me to say 'don't'. But I will not. I am merely going to say, '*Before* you criticise them, read one of the classics of American journalism, "Father Forgets."' It originally appeared as an editorial in the *People's Home Journal*. We are reprinting it here with the author's permission, as condensed in the *Reader's Digest:*

'Father Forgets' is one of those little pieces which—dashed off in a moment of sincere feeling—strikes an echoing chord in so many readers as to become a perennial reprint favourite. 'Since its first appearance, "Father Forgets" has been reproduced, writes the author, W. Livingstone Larned, "in hundreds of magazines and house organs, and in newspapers the country over. It has been reprinted almost as extensively in many foreign languages. I have given personal permission to thousands who wished to read it from school, church and lecture platforms. It has been "on the air" on countless occasions and programmes. Oddly enough, college periodicals have used it, and high-school magazines. Sometimes a little piece seems mysteriously to "click". This one certainly did.'

FATHER FORGETS

W. LIVINGSTON LARNED

Listen, son: I am saying this as you lie asleep, one little paw crumpled under your cheek and the blond curls stickily wet on your damp forehead. I have stolen into your room alone. Just a few minutes ago, as I sat reading my paper in the library, a stifling wave of remorse swept over me. Guiltily I came to your bedside.

There are the things I was thinking, son: I had been cross to you. I scolded you as you were dressing for school because you gave your face merely a dab with a towel. I took you to task for not cleaning your shoes. I called out angrily when you threw some of your things on the floor.

At breakfast I found fault, too. You spilled things. You gulped down your food. You put your elbows on the table. You spread butter too thick on your bread. And as you started off to play and I made for my train, you turned and waved a hand and called, 'Goodbye, Daddy!' and I frowned, and said in reply, 'Hold your shoulders back!'

Then it began all over again in the late afternoon. As I came up the road I spied you, down on your knees, playing marbles. There were holes in your stockings. I humiliated you before your boyfriends by marching you ahead of me to the house. Stockings were expensive—and if you had to buy them you would be more careful! Imagine that, son, from a father!

Do you remember, later, when I was reading in the library, how you came in timidly, with a sort of hurt look in your eyes? When I glanced up over my paper, impatient at the interruption, you hesitated at the door. 'What is it you want?' I snapped.

You said nothing, but ran across in one tempestuous plunge, and threw your arms around my neck and kissed me, and your small arms tightened with an affection that God had set blooming in your heart and which even neglect could not wither. And then you were gone, pattering up the stairs.

Well, son, it was shortly afterwards that my paper slipped from my hands and a terrible sickening fear came over me. What has habit been doing to me? The habit of finding fault, of reprimanding—this was my reward to you for being a boy. It was not that I did not love you; it was that I expected too much of youth. I was measuring you by the yardstick of my own years.

And there was so much that was good and fine and true in your character. The little heart of you was as big as the dawn itself over the wide hills. This was shown by your spontaneous impulse to rush in and kiss me good night. Nothing else matters tonight, son. I have come to your bedside in the darkness, and I have knelt there, ashamed!

It is a feeble atonement; I know you would not understand these things if I told them to you during your waking hours. But tomorrow I will be a real daddy! I will chum with you, and suffer when you suffer, and laugh when you laugh. I will bite my tongue when impatient words come. I will keep saying as if it were a ritual: 'He is nothing but a boy—a little boy!'

I am afraid I have visualised you as a man. Yet as I see you now, son, crumpled and weary in your cot, I see that you are still a baby. Yesterday you were in your mother's arms, your head on her shoulder. I have asked too much, too much.

Instead of condemning people, let's try to understand them. Let's try to figure out why they do what they do. That's a lot more profitable and intriguing than criticism; and it breeds sympathy, tolerance and kindness. 'To know all is to forgive all.'

As Dr Johnson said, 'God himself, sir, does not propose to judge man until the end of his days.'

Why should you and I?

POINTS TO REMEMBER:

1. The futility of criticism.
2. Aim to change yourself first, and then others.
3. Parental guide on correcting children.

12

IF YOU'RE WRONG, ADMIT IT

Within a minute's walk of my house there was a wild stretch of virgin timber, where the blackberry thickets foamed white in the springtime, where the squirrels nested and reared their young, and the horse weeds grew as tall as a horse's head. This unspoiled woodland was called Forest Park—and it was a forest, probably not much different in appearance from what it was when Columbus discovered America. I frequently walked in this park with Rex, my little Boston bulldog. He was a friendly, harmless little hound; and since we rarely met anyone in the park, I took Rex along without a leash or a muzzle.

One day we encountered a mounted policeman in the park, a policeman itching to show his authority.

'What do you mean by letting that dog run loose in the park without a muzzle and leash?' he reprimanded me. 'Don't you know it's against the law?'

'Yes, I know it is,' I replied softly, 'but I didn't think he would do any harm out here.'

'You didn't think! You didn't think! The law doesn't give a tinker's damn about what you think. That dog might kill a squirrel or bite a child. Now, I'm going to let you off this time; but if I catch this dog out here again without a muzzle and a leash, you'll have to tell it to the judge.'

I meekly promised to obey.

And I did obey—for a few times. But Rex didn't like the muzzle, and neither did I; so we decided to take a chance. Everything was lovely for a while, and then we struck a snag. Rex and I raced over the brow of a hill one afternoon and there, suddenly—to my dismay—I saw the majesty of the law, astride a bay horse. Rex was out in front, heading straight for the officer.

I was in for it. I knew it. So I didn't wait until the policeman started talking. I beat him to it. I said: 'Officer, you've caught me red-handed. I'm guilty. I have no alibis, no excuses. You warned me last week that if I brought the dog out here again without a muzzle you would fine me.'

'Well, now,' the policeman responded in a soft tone. 'I know it's a temptation to let a little dog like that have a run out here when nobody is around.'

'Sure it's a temptation,' I replied, 'but it is against the law.'

'Well, a little dog like that isn't going to harm anybody,' the policeman remonstrated.

'No, but he may kill squirrels,' I said.

'Well now, I think you are taking this a bit too seriously,' he told me. 'I'll tell you what you do. You just let him run over the hill there where I can't see him—and we'll forget all about it.'

That policeman, being human, wanted a feeling of importance; so when I began to condemn myself, the only way he could nourish his self-esteem was to take the magnanimous attitude of showing mercy.

But suppose I had tried to defend myself—well, did you ever argue with a policeman?

But instead of breaking lances with him, I admitted that he was absolutely right and I was absolutely wrong; I admitted it quickly, openly and with enthusiasm. The affair terminated graciously in my taking his side and his taking my side. Lord Chesterfield himself could hardly have been more gracious than this mounted policeman, who, only a week previously, had threatened to have the law on me.

If we know we are going to be rebuked anyhow, isn't it far better to beat the other person to it and do it ourselves? Isn't it much easier to listen to self-criticism than to bear condemnation from alien lips?

CHARGE AHEAD WITH COURAGE

Say about yourself all the derogatory things you know the other person is thinking or wants to say or intends to say—and say them before that person has a chance to say them. The chances are a hundred to one that a generous, forgiving attitude will be taken and your mistakes will be minimised just as the mounted policeman did with me and Rex.

Ferdinand E. Warren, a commercial artist, used this technique to win the goodwill of a petulant, scolding buyer of art.

'It is important, in making drawings for advertising and publishing purposes, to be precise and very exact,' Mr Warren said as he told the story.

'Some art editors demand that their commissions be executed immediately; and in these cases, some slight error is liable to occur. I knew one art director in particular who was always delighted to find fault with some little thing. I have often left his office in disgust, not because of the criticism, but because of his method of attack. Recently I delivered a rush job to this editor, and he phoned me to call at his office immediately. He said something was wrong. When I arrived, I found just what I had anticipated—and dreaded. He was hostile, gloating over his chance to criticise. He demanded with heat why I had done so and so. My opportunity had come to apply the self-criticism I had been studying about. So I said, "Mr So-and-so, if what you say is true, I am at fault and there is absolutely no excuse for my blunder. I have been doing drawings for you long enough to know better, I'm ashamed of myself."

'Immediately he started to defend me, "Yes, you're right, but after all, this isn't a serious mistake. It is only—"

'I interrupted him. "Any mistake," I said, "may be costly and they are all irritating."

'He started to break in, but I wouldn't let him. I was having a grand time. For the first time in my life, I was criticising myself—and I loved it.

'"I should have been more careful," I continued. "You give me a lot of work, and you deserve the best; so I'm going to do this drawing all over."

'"No! No!" he protested. "I wouldn't think of putting you to all that trouble." He praised my work, assured me that he wanted only a minor change and that my slight error hadn't cost his firm any money; and, after all, it was a mere detail—not worth worrying about.

'My eagerness to criticise myself took all the fight out of him. He ended up by taking me to lunch; and before we parted, he gave me a cheque and another commission.'

There is a certain degree of satisfaction in having the courage to admit one's errors. It not only clears the air of guilt and defensiveness, but often helps solve the problem created by the error.

Bruce Harvey of Albuquerque, New Mexico, had incorrectly authorised payment of full wages to an employee on sick leave. When he discovered his error, he brought it to the attention of the employee and explained that to correct the mistake he would have to reduce his next paycheque by the entire amount of the overpayment. The employee pleaded that as that would cause him a serious financial problem, could the money be repaid over a period of time? In order to do this, Harvey explained, he would have to obtain his supervisor's approval. 'And this I knew,' reported Harvey, 'would result in a boss-type explosion. While trying to decide how to handle this situation better, I realised that the whole mess was my fault and I would have to admit it to my boss.

'I walked into his office, told him that I had made a mistake and then informed him of the complete facts. He replied in an explosive manner that it was the fault of the personnel department. I repeated that it was my fault. He exploded again about carelessness in the accounting department. Again, I explained it was my fault. He blamed two other people in the office. But each time I reiterated it was my fault. Finally, he looked at me and said, "Okay, it was your fault. Now straighten it out." The error was corrected and nobody got into trouble. I felt great because I was able to handle a tense situation and had the courage not to seek alibis. My boss has had more respect for me ever since.'

Any fool can try to defend his or her mistakes—and most fools do—but it raises one above the herd and gives one a feeling of nobility and exultation to admit one's mistakes.

POINTS TO REMEMBER:

1. The universal need to feel important.
2. It is much easier to condemn yourself than giving others a chance to do so.
3. You can earn other people's respect by admitting to your mistakes.

13

HOW TO ANALYSE AND SOLVE WORRY PROBLEMS

Will Any Magic FORMULA solve *all* worry problems? No, of course not.

Then what *is* the answer? The answer is that we must equip ourselves to deal with different kinds of worries by learning the three basic steps of problem analysis. The three steps are:

1. Get the facts.
2. Analyse the facts.
3. Arrive at a decision—and then act on that decision.

Obvious stuff? Yes, Aristotle taught it—and used it. And you and I must use it too if we are going to solve the problems that are harassing us and turning our days and nights into veritable hells.

Let's take the first rule:

GET THE FACTS

Why is it so important to get the facts? Because unless we have the facts we can't possibly even attempt to solve our problem intelligently. Without the facts, all we can do is stew around in confusion. My idea? No, that was the idea of the late Herbert E. Hawkes, Dean of Columbia College, Columbia University, for twenty-two years. He had helped two hundred thousand students solve their worry problems; and he told me that *'confusion is the chief cause of worry.'* He put it this way—he said, 'Half the worry in the world is caused by people trying to make decisions before they have sufficient knowledge on which to base a decision. For example,' he said, 'if I have a problem which has to be faced at three o'clock next Tuesday, I refuse to even try to make a decision about it until next Tuesday arrives. In the meantime, I concentrate on getting all the facts that bear on the problem. I don't worry,' he said. 'I don't agonize over my problem. I don't lose any sleep. I simply concentrate on getting the facts. And by the time Tuesday rolls around, if I've got all the facts, the problem usually solves itself!'

I asked Dean Hawkes if this meant he had licked worry entirely. 'Yes,' he said, 'I think I can honestly say that my life is now almost totally devoid of worry. I have found,' he went on, 'that if a man will devote his time to securing facts in an impartial, objective way, his worries will usually evaporate in the light of knowledge.'

Let me repeat that: "If a man will devote his time to securing facts in an impartial, objective way, his worries will usually evaporate in the light of knowledge."

But what do most of us do? If we bother with facts at all—and Thomas Edison said in all seriousness, 'There is no expedient to which a man will not resort to avoid the labour of thinking'—if we bother with facts at all, we hunt like bird dogs after the facts that bolster up what we *already* think—and ignore all the others! We want only the facts that justify our acts—the facts that fit in conveniently with our wishful thinking and justify our preconceived prejudices!

Is it any wonder, then, that we find it so hard to get at the answers to our problems? Wouldn't we have the same trouble trying to solve a second-grade arithmetic problem, if we went ahead on the assumption that two plus two equals five? Yet there are a lot of people in this world who make life a hell for themselves and others by insisting that two plus two equals five—or maybe five hundred!

What can we do about it? We have to keep our emotions out of our thinking; and, as Dean Hawkes put it, we must secure the facts in 'an impartial, objective' manner. That is not an easy task when we are worried. When we are worried, our emotions are riding high. But here are two ideas that I have found helpful when trying to step aside from my problems, in order to see the facts in a clear, objective manner.

When trying to get the facts, I pretend that I am collecting this information not for myself, but for some other person. This helps me to take a cold, impartial view of the evidence. This helps me eliminate my emotions.

While trying to collect the facts about the problem that is worrying me, I sometimes pretend that I am a lawyer preparing to argue the other side of the issue. In other words, I try to get all the facts against myself—all the facts that are damaging to my wishes, all the facts I don't like to face.

Then I write down both my side of the case and the other side of the case—and I generally find that the truth lies somewhere in between these two extremities.

Here is the point I am trying to make. Neither you, nor I, nor Einstein, nor the Supreme Court of the United States is brilliant enough to reach an intelligent decision on any problem without first getting the facts. Thomas Edison knew that. At the time of his death, he had two thousand five hundred notebooks filled with facts about the problems he was facing.

So Rule 1 for solving our problems is: *Get the facts.* Let's do what Dean Hawkes did—let's not even attempt to solve our problems without first collecting all the facts in an impartial manner.

However, getting all the facts in the world won't do us any good until we analyse them and interpret them.

I have found from costly experience that it is much easier to analyse the facts after writing them down. In fact, merely writing the facts on a piece of paper and stating our problem clearly goes a long way toward helping us reach a sensible decision. As Charles Kettering puts it, "A problem well stated is a problem half solved."

Let me show you all this as it works out in practice. Since the Chinese say one picture is worth ten thousand words, suppose I show you a picture of how one man put exactly what we are talking about into concrete action.

THE LITCHFIELD METHOD

Let's take the case of Galen Litchfield—a man I have known for several years; one of the most successful American businessmen in the Far East. Mr Litchfield was in China in 1942, when the Japanese invaded Shanghai. And here is his story as he told it to me while a guest in my home, 'Shortly after the Japs took Pearl Harbour,' Galen Litchfield began, 'they came swarming into Shanghai. I was the manager of the Asia Life Insurance Company in Shanghai. They sent us an "army liquidator"—he was really an admiral—and gave me orders to assist this man in liquidating our assets. I didn't have any choice in the matter. I could co-operate—or else. And the "or else" was certain death.

'I went through the motions of doing what I was told, because I had no alternative. But there was one block of securities, worth $750,000, which I left off the list I gave to the admiral. I left that block of securities off the list because they belonged to our Hong Kong organization and had nothing to do with the Shanghai assets. All the same, I feared I might be in hot water if the Japs found out what I had done. And they soon found out.

'I wasn't in the office when the discovery was made, but my head accountant was there. He told me that the Jap admiral flew into a rage, and stamped and swore, and called me a thief and a traitor! I had defied the Japanese army! I knew what that meant. I would be thrown into the Bridgehouse!

'The Bridgehouse! The torture chamber of the Japanese Gestapo! I had had personal friends who had killed themselves rather than be taken to that prison. I had had other friends who had died in that place after ten days of questioning and torture. Now I was slated for the Bridgehouse myself!

'What did I do? I heard the news on Sunday afternoon. I suppose I should have been terrified. And I would have been terrified if I hadn't had a definite technique for solving my problems. For years, whenever I was worried I had always gone to my typewriter and written down two questions—and the answers to these questions:

'*1. What am I worrying about?*
'*2. What can I do about it?*

'I used to try to answer those questions without writing them down. But I stopped that years ago. I found that writing down both the questions and the answers clarifies my thinking. So, that Sunday afternoon, I went directly to my room at the Shanghai YMCA, and got out my typewriter. I wrote:

'I. What am I worrying about?

'I am afraid I will be thrown into the Bridgehouse tomorrow morning.

'Then I typed out the second question:

'2. What can I do about it?

'I spent hours thinking out and writing down the four courses of action I could take—and what the probable consequence of each action would be.

'I can try to explain to the Japanese admiral. But he "no speak English". If I try to explain to him through an interpreter, I may stir him up again. That might mean death, for he is cruel and would rather dump me in the Bridgehouse than bother talking about it.

'I can try to escape. Impossible. They keep track of me all the time. I have to check in and out of my room at the YMCA. If I try to escape, I'll probably be captured and shot.

'I can stay here in my room and not go near the office again. If I do, the Japanese admiral will be suspicious, will probably send soldiers to get me and throw me into the Bridgehouse without giving me a chance to say a word.

'I can go down to the office as usual on Monday morning. If I do, there is a chance that the Japanese admiral may be so busy that he will not think of what I did. Even if he does think of it, he may have cooled off and may not bother me. If this happens, I am all right. Even if he does bother me, I'll still have a chance to try to explain to him. So, going down to the office as usual on Monday morning, and acting as if nothing had gone wrong, gives me two chances to escape the Bridgehouse.

'As soon as I thought it all out and decided to accept the fourth plan—to go down to the office as usual on Monday morning—I felt immensely relieved.

'When I entered the office the next morning, the Japanese admiral sat there with a cigarette dangling from his mouth.

He glared at me as he always did; and said nothing. Six weeks later—thank God—he went back to Tokyo and my worries were ended.

'As I have already said, I probably saved my life by sitting down that Sunday afternoon and writing out all the various steps I could take and then writing down the probable consequence of each step and calmly coming to a decision. If I hadn't done that, I might have floundered and hesitated and done the wrong thing on the spur of the moment. If I hadn't thought out my problem and come to a decision, I would have been frantic with worry all Sunday afternoon. I wouldn't have slept that night. I would have gone down to the office Monday morning with a harassed and worried look; and that alone might have aroused the suspicion of the Japanese admiral and spurred him to act.

'Experience has proved to me, time after time, the enormous value of arriving at a decision. It is the failure to arrive at a fixed purpose, the inability to stop going round and round in maddening circles, that drives men to nervous breakdowns and living hells. I find that 50 per cent of my worries vanish once I arrive at a clear, definite decision; and another 40 per cent usually vanishes once I start to carry out that decision.

'So I banish about 90 per cent of my worries by taking these four steps:

'1. Writing down precisely what I am worrying about.
'2. Writing down what I can do about it.
'3. Deciding what to do.
'4. Starting immediately to carry out that decision.'

Galen Litchfield is now the Far Eastern Director for Starr, Park and Freeman, Inc., 111 John Street, New York, representing large insurance and financial interests.

In fact, as I said before, Galen Litchfield today is one of

the most important American businessmen in Asia; and he confessed to me that he owes a large part of his success to this method of analysing worry and meeting it head-on.

Why is his method so superb? Because it is efficient, concrete and goes directly to the heart of the problem. On top of all that, it is climaxed by the third and indispensable rule: *do something about it.* Unless we carry out our action, all our fact-finding and analysis is whistling upwind—it's a sheer waste of energy.

William James said this, 'When once a decision is reached and execution is the order of the day, dismiss absolutely all responsibility and care about the outcome.' (In this case, William James undoubtedly used the word 'care' as a synonym for 'anxiety.') He meant—once you have made a careful decision based on facts, *go* into action. Don't stop to reconsider. Don't begin to hesitate, worry and retrace your steps. Don't lose yourself in self-doubting which begets other doubts. Don't keep looking back over your shoulder.

Why don't you employ Galen Litchfield's technique to one of your worries right now?

Here is question No. 1—*What am I worrying about?*
Question No. 2—*What can I do about It?*
Question No. 3—Here is what I am going to do about it.
Question No. 4—When am I going to start doing it?

POINTS TO REMEMBER:

1. Equip yourself to deal with all kinds of troubles.
2. The three steps required to analyse a problem.
3. Galen Litchfield's method to tackle a problem.

14

FOUR GOOD WORKING HABITS THAT WILL HELP PREVENT FATIGUE AND WORRY

Good Working Habit No. 1: Clear Your Desk of All Papers Except Those Relating to the Immediate Problem at Hand.

Roland L. Williams, President of Chicago and Northwestern Railway, says, 'A person with his desk piled high with papers on various matters will find his work much easier and more accurate if he clears that desk of all but the immediate problem on hand. I call this good housekeeping, and it is the number-one step toward efficiency.'

If you visit the Library of Congress in Washington, D.C., you will find five words painted on the ceiling—five words written by the poet Pope,

"Order is Heaven's first law."

Order ought to be the first law of business, too. But is it? No, the average businessman's desk is cluttered up with papers that he hasn't looked at for weeks. In fact, the publisher of a New Orleans newspaper once told me that his secretary cleared up one of his desks and found a typewriter that had been missing for two years!

The mere sight of a desk littered with unanswered mail

and reports and memos is enough to breed confusion, tension and worries. It is much worse than that. The constant reminder of 'a million things to do and no time to do them' can worry you not only into tension and fatigue, but it can also worry you into high blood pressure, heart trouble and stomach ulcers.

Dr. John H. Stokes, professor, Graduate School of Medicine, University of Pennsylvania, read a paper before the National Convention of the American Medical Association—a paper entitled 'Functional Neuroses as Complications of Organic Disease'. In that paper, Dr. Stokes listed eleven conditions under the title 'What to Look for in the Patient's State of Mind'. Here is the first item on that list,

'The sense of must or obligation; the unending stretch of things ahead that simply have to be done.'

But how can such an elementary procedure as clearing your desk and making decisions help you avoid this high pressure, this sense of *must*, this sense of an 'unending stretch of things ahead that simply have to be done'? Dr. William L. Sadler, the famous psychiatrist, tells of a patient who, by using this simple device, avoided a nervous breakdown. The man was an executive in a big Chicago firm. When he came to Dr. Sadler's office, he was tense, nervous and worried. He knew he was heading for a tailspin, but he couldn't quit work. He had to have help.

'While this man was telling me his story,' Dr. Sadler says, 'my telephone rang. It was the hospital calling; and, instead of deferring the matter, I took time right then to come to a decision. I always settle questions, if possible, right on the spot. I had no sooner hung up than the phone rang again. Again, an urgent matter, which I took time to discuss. The third interruption came when a colleague of mine came to my office for advice on a patient who was critically ill. When I had finished with him, I turned to my caller and began to apologize for keeping him waiting. But he had brightened up. He had a completely different look on his face.'

'Don't apologize, doctor!' this man said to Sadler. 'In the last ten minutes, I think I've got a hunch as to what is wrong with me. I'm going back to my office and revising my working habits.... But before I go, do you mind if I take a look in your desk?'

Dr. Sadler opened up the drawers of his desk. All empty—except for supplies. 'Tell me,' said the patient, 'where do you keep your unfinished business?'

'Finished!' said Sadler.

'And where do you keep your unanswered mail?'

'Answered!' Sadler told him. 'My rule is never to lay down a letter until I have answered it. I dictate the reply to my secretary at once.'

Six weeks later, this same executive invited Dr. Sadler to come to his office. He was changed—and so was his desk. He opened the desk drawers to show there was no unfinished business inside of the desk. 'Six weeks ago,' this executive said, 'I had three different desks in two different offices—and was snowed under by my work. I was never finished. After talking to you, I came back here and cleared out a wagonload of reports and old papers. Now I work at one desk, settle things as they come up and don't have a mountain of unfinished business nagging at me and making me tense and worried. But the most astonishing thing is I've recovered completely. There is nothing wrong any more with my health!'

Charles Evans Hughes, former Chief Justice of the United States Supreme Court, said, 'Men do not die from overwork. They die from dissipation and worry.' Yes, from the dissipation of their energies—and worry because they never seem to get their work done.

Good Working Habit No. 2: Do Things in the Order of Their Importance.

Henry L. Doherty, Founder of the nation-wide Cities Service Company, said that regardless of how much salary he paid, there were two abilities he found it almost impossible to find.

Those two priceless abilities are: first, the ability to think. Second, the ability to do things in the order of their importance.

Charles Luckman, the lad who started from scratch and climbed in twelve years to president of the Pepsodent Company, got a salary of a hundred thousand dollars a year and made a million dollars besides—that lad declares that he owes much of his success to developing the two abilities that Henry L. Doherty said he found almost impossible to find. Charles Luckman said, 'As far back as I can remember, I have gotten up at five o'clock in the morning because I can think better then, than any other time—I can think better then and plan my day, plan to do things in the order of their importance.'

Franklin Bettger, one of America's most successful insurance salesmen, doesn't wait until five o'clock in the morning to plan his day. He plans it the night before—sets a goal for himself—a goal to sell a certain amount of insurance that day. If he fails, that amount is added to the next day—and so on.

I know from long experience that one is not always able to do things in the order of their importance, but I also know that some kind of plan to do first things first is infinitely better than extemporizing as you go along.

If George Bernard Shaw had not made it a rigid rule to do first things first, he would probably have failed as a writer and might have remained a bank cashier all his life. His plan called for writing five pages each day. That plan inspired him to go right on writing five pages a day for nine heart-breaking years, even though he made a total of only thirty dollars in those nine years—about a penny a day. Even Robinson Crusoe wrote out a schedule of what he would do each hour of the day.

Good Working Habit No. 3: When You Face a Problem, Solve It Then and There if You Have the Facts Necessary to Make a Decision. Don't Keep Putting off Decisions.

One of my former students, the late H. P. Howell, told me that when he was a member of the board of directors of U. S. Steel, the meetings of the board were often long-drawn-out affairs—many problems were discussed, few decisions were made. The result: each member of the board had to carry home bundles of reports to study.

Finally, Mr Howell persuaded the board of directors to take up one problem at a time and come to a decision. No procrastination—no putting off. The decision might be to ask for additional facts; it might be to do something or do nothing. But a decision was reached on each problem before passing on to the next. Mr Howell told me that the results were striking and salutary: the docket was cleared. The calendar was clean. No longer was it necessary for each member to carry home a bundle of reports. No longer was there a worried sense of unresolved problems.

A good rule, not only for the board of directors of U. S. Steel, but for you and me.

Good Working Habit No. 4: Learn to Organize, Deputize, and Supervise.

Many a businessman is driving himself to a premature grave because he has never learned to delegate responsibility to others and insists on doing everything himself. Result: details and confusion overwhelm him. He is driven by a sense of hurry, worry, anxiety and tension. It is hard to learn to delegate responsibilities. I know. It was hard for me, awfully hard. I also know from experience the disasters that can be caused by delegating authority to the wrong people. But difficult as it is to delegate authority, the executive must do it if he is to avoid worry, tension and fatigue.

The man who builds up a big business, and doesn't learn to organize, deputize and supervise, usually pops off with heart trouble in his fifties or early sixties—heart trouble caused by tension and worries. Want a specific instance? Look at the death notices in your local paper.

POINTS TO REMEMBER:

1. Being organised will make you more productive.
2. Do things in the order of their importance.
3. Don't keep putting off taking decisions.

15

DO THIS—AND CRITICISM CAN'T HURT YOU

I realize now that people are not thinking about you and me or caring what is said about us. They are thinking about themselves—before breakfast, after breakfast and right on until ten minutes past midnight. They would be a thousand times more concerned about a slight headache of their own than they would about the news of your death or mine.

Even if you and I are lied about, ridiculed, double-crossed, knifed in the back and sold down the river by one out of every six of our most intimate friends—let's not indulge in an orgy of self-pity. Instead, let's remind ourselves that that's precisely what happened to Jesus. One of His twelve most intimate friends turned traitor for a bribe that would amount, in our modern money, to about nineteen dollars. Another one of His twelve most intimate friends openly deserted Jesus the moment He got into trouble, and declared three times that he didn't even know Jesus—and he swore as he said it. One out of six! That is what happened to Jesus. Why should you and I expect a better score?

I discovered years ago that although I couldn't keep people from criticizing me unjustly, I could do something infinitely more important: I could determine whether I would let the unjust condemnation disturb me.

Let's be clear about this: I am not advocating ignoring all criticism. Far from it. I am talking about *ignoring only unjust criticism.*

When Charles Schwab was addressing the student body at Princeton, he confessed that one of the most important lessons he had ever learned was taught to him by an old German who worked in Schwab's steel mill. This old German got involved in a hot wartime argument with the other steelworkers, and they tossed him into the river. 'When he came into my office,' Mr. Schwab said, 'covered with mud and water, I asked him what he had said to the men who had thrown him into the river, and he replied, "I yust laughed."'

Mr. Schwab declared that he had adopted that old German's words as his motto, 'Yust laugh.'

That motto is especially good when you are the victim of unjust criticism. You can answer the man who answers you back, but what can you say to the man who 'yust laughs'?

Lincoln might have broken under the strain of the Civil War if he hadn't learned the folly of trying to answer all the vitriolic condemnations hurled at him. His description of how he handled his critics has become a literary gem—a classic. General MacArthur had a copy of it hanging above his headquarters desk during the war; and Winston Churchill has a framed copy of it on the walls of his study at Chartwell. It goes like this, 'If I were to try to read, much less to answer, all the attacks made on me, this shop might as well be closed for any other business. I do the very best I know how—the very best I can; and I mean to keep on doing so until the end. If the end brings me out all right, then what is said against me won't matter. If the ends brings me out wrong, then ten angels swearing I was right would make no difference.'

POINTS TO REMEMBER:

1. People are constantly thinking about themselves.
2. Don't let unjust criticism affect you.
3. If anything bad happens, laugh it out.

16

FOOL THINGS I HAVE DONE

I have a folder in my private filing cabinet marked 'FTD'—short for 'Fool Things I Have Done'. I put in that folder written records of the fool things I have been guilty of. I sometimes dictate these memos to my secretary, but sometimes they are so personal, so stupid, that I am ashamed to dictate them, so I write them out in longhand.

I can still recall some of the criticisms that I put in my 'FTD' folders fifteen years ago. If I had been utterly honest with myself, I would now have a filing cabinet bursting out at the seams with these 'FTD' memos. I can truthfully repeat what King Saul said thirty centuries ago, 'I have played the fool and have erred exceedingly.'

When I get out my 'FTD' folders and reread the criticisms I have written of myself, they help me deal with the toughest problem I shall ever face: the management of Dale Carnegie.

I used to blame my troubles on other people; but as I have grown older—and wiser, I hope—I have realized that I myself, in the last analysis, am to blame for almost all my misfortunes. Lots of people have discovered that, as they grow older. 'No one but myself,' said Napoleon at St. Helena, 'no one but myself can be blamed for my fall. I have been my own greatest enemy—the cause of my own disastrous fate.'

Walt Whitman put it this way, 'Have you learned lessons only of those who admired you, and were tender with you, and stood aside for you? Have you not learned great lessons from those who rejected you, and braced themselves against you, or disputed the passage with you?'

Instead of waiting for our enemies to criticize us or our work, let's beat them to it. Let's be our own most severe critic. Let's find and remedy all our weaknesses before our enemies get a chance to say a word. That is what Charles Darwin did. In fact, he spent fifteen years criticizing—well, the story goes like this: when Darwin completed the manuscript of his immortal book, *On The Origin of Species,* he realized that the publication of his revolutionary concept of creation would rock the intellectual and religious worlds. So he *became his own critic and spent another fifteen years, checking his data, challenging his reasoning, criticizing his conclusions.*

Suppose someone denounced you as 'a damn fool'—what would you do? Get angry? Indignant? Here is what Lincoln did: Edward M. Stanton, Lincoln's Secretary of War, once called Lincoln 'a damn fool'. Stanton was indignant because Lincoln had been meddling in Stanton's affairs. In order to please a selfish politician, Lincoln had signed an order transferring certain regiments. Stanton not only refused to carry out Lincoln's orders, but swore that Lincoln was a damn fool for ever signing such orders. What happened? When Lincoln was told what Stanton had said, Lincoln calmly replied, 'If Stanton said I am a damned fool, then I must be, for he is nearly always right. I'll just step over and see for myself.'

Lincoln did go to see Stanton. Stanton convinced him that the order was wrong and Lincoln withdrew it. Lincoln welcomed criticism when he knew it was sincere, founded on knowledge and given in a spirit of helpfulness.

You and I ought to welcome that kind of criticism, too, for we can't even hope to be right more than three times out of four. At least, that was all Theodore Roosevelt said he could hope for, when he was in the White House. Einstein, the most profound thinker now living, confesses that his conclusions are wrong ninety-nine per cent of the time!

'The opinions of our enemies,' said La Rochefoucauld, 'come nearer to the truth about us than do our own opinions.'

I know that statement may be true many times; yet when anyone starts to criticize me, if I do not watch myself, I instantly and automatically leap to the defensive—even before I have the slightest idea what my critic is going to say. I am disgusted with myself every time I do it. We all tend to resent criticism and lap up praise, regardless of whether either the criticism or the praise is justified. We are not creatures of logic. We are creatures of emotions. Our logic is like a birch-bark canoe tossed about on a deep, dark, stormy sea of emotion.

If we hear that someone has spoken ill of us, let's not try to defend ourselves. Every fool does that. Let's be original—and humble—and brilliant! Let's confound our critic and win applause for ourselves by saying, 'If my critic had known about *all my other faults*, he would have criticized me much more severely than he did.'

Here is another idea: when your anger is rising because you feel you have been unjustly condemned, why not stop and say, 'Just a minute... I am far from perfect. If Einstein admits he is wrong 99 per cent of the time, maybe I am wrong at least 80 per cent of the time. Maybe I deserve this criticism. If I do, I ought to be thankful for it, and try to profit by it.

POINTS TO REMEMBER:

1. Develop the ability of healthy self-criticism.
2. No one but you are to be blamed for your fall.
3. Sometimes the criticisms of your enemies tell the truest things about you.

17

REMEMBER THAT NO ONE EVER KICKS A DEAD DOG

An event occurred in 1929 that created a national sensation in educational circles. Learned men from all over America rushed to Chicago to witness the affair. A few years earlier, a young man by the name of Robert Hutchins had worked his way through Yale, acting as a waiter, a lumberjack, a tutor and a clothesline salesman. Now, only eight years later, he was being inaugurated as president of the fourth richest university in America, the University of Chicago. His age? Thirty. Incredible! The older educators shook their heads. Criticism came roaring down upon this 'boy wonder' like a rockslide. He was this and he was that—too young, inexperienced—his educational ideas were cockeyed. Even the newspapers joined in the attack.

The day he was inaugurated, a friend said to the father of Robert Maynard Hutchins, 'I was shocked this morning to read that newspaper editorial denouncing your son.'

'Yes,' the elder Hutchins replied, 'it was severe, but remember that no one ever kicks a dead dog.'

Yes, and the more important a dog is, the more satisfaction people get in kicking him. The Prince of Wales who later became Edward VIII (now the Duke of Windsor) had that brought home to him in the seat of his pants. He was attending Dartmouth College in Devonshire at the time—a college that corresponds to our Naval Academy at Annapolis. The Prince was about fourteen. One day one of the naval officers found him crying, and asked him what was wrong. He refused to tell at first, but finally admitted the truth: he was being kicked by the naval cadets. The commodore of the college summoned the boys and explained to them that the Prince had not complained, but he wanted to find out why the Prince had been singled out for this rough treatment.

After much hemming and hawing and toe scraping, the cadets finally confessed that when they themselves became commanders and captains in the King's Navy, they wanted to be able to say that they had kicked the King!

So when you are kicked and criticized, remember that it is often done because it gives the kicker a feeling of importance. It often means that you are accomplishing something and are worthy of attention. Many people get a sense of savage satisfaction out of denouncing those who are better educated than they are or more successful. For example, while I was writing this chapter, I received a letter from a woman denouncing General William Booth, founder of the Salvation Army. I had given a laudatory broadcast about General Booth; so this woman wrote me, saying that General Booth had stolen eight million dollars of the money he had collected to help poor people. The charge, of course, was absurd. But this woman wasn't looking for truth. She was seeking the mean-spirited gratification that she got from tearing down someone far above her. I threw her bitter letter into the wastebasket, and thanked Almighty God that I wasn't married to her. Her letter didn't tell me anything at all about General Booth, but it did tell me a lot about her. Schopenhauer had said it years ago, 'Vulgar people take huge delight in the faults and follies of great men.'

One hardly thinks of the president of Yale as a vulgar man; yet a former president of Yale, Timothy Dwight, apparently took huge delight in denouncing a man who was running for president of the United States. The president of Yale warned that if this man were elected president, 'we may see our wives and daughters the victims of legal prostitution, soberly dishonoured, speciously polluted; the outcasts of delicacy and virtue, the loathing of God and man.'

Sounds almost like a denunciation of Hitler, doesn't it? But it wasn't. It was a denunciation of Thomas Jefferson. *Which* Thomas Jefferson? Surely not the *immortal* Thomas Jefferson, the author of the Declaration of Independence, the patron saint of democracy? Yea, verily, that was the man.

What American do you suppose was denounced as a 'hypocrite', 'an impostor' and as 'little better than a murderer'? A newspaper cartoon depicted him on a guillotine, the big knife ready to cut off his head. Crowds jeered at him and hissed him as he rode through the streets. Who was he? George Washington.

But that occurred a long time ago. Maybe human nature has improved since then. Let's see. Let's take the case of Admiral Peary—the explorer who startled and thrilled the world by reaching the North Pole with dog sleds on April 6, 1909—a goal that brave men for centuries had suffered and starved and died to attain. Peary himself almost died from cold and starvation; and eight of his toes were frozen so hard they had to be cut off. He was so overwhelmed with disasters that he feared he would go insane. His superior naval officers in Washington were burned up because Peary was getting so much publicity and acclaim. So they accused him of collecting money for scientific expeditions and then 'lying around and loafing in the Arctic'.

And they probably believed it because it is almost impossible not to believe what you want to believe. Their determination to humiliate and block Peary was so violent that only a direct order from President McKinley enabled Peary to continue his career in the Arctic.

Would Peary have been denounced if he had had a desk job in the Navy Department in Washington? No. He wouldn't have been important enough then to have aroused jealousy.

General Grant had an even worse experience than Admiral Peary. In 1862, General Grant won the first great decisive victory that the North had enjoyed—a victory that was achieved in one afternoon, a victory that made Grant a national idol overnight—a victory that had tremendous repercussions even in far-off Europe—a victory that set church bells ringing and bonfires blazing from Maine to the banks of the Mississippi. Yet within six weeks after achieving that great victory, Grant—hero of the North—was *arrested and his army was taken from him. He wept with humiliation and despair.*

Why was General U. S. Grant arrested at the flood tide of his victory? Largely because he had aroused the jealousy and envy of his arrogant superiors.

If we are tempted to be worried about unjust criticism, here is a rule:

REMEMBER THAT UNJUST CRITICISM IS OFTEN A DISGUISED COMPLIMENT. REMEMBER THAT NO ONE EVER KICKS A DEAD DOG.

POINTS TO REMEMBER:

1. The more you succeed, the more enemies you will make.
2. People often try to bring others down in order to feel important.
3. Recognize the compliment behind the criticism.

18

WOULD YOU TAKE A MILLION DOLLARS FOR WHAT YOU HAVE?

Time ran an article about a sergeant who had been wounded on Guadalcanal. Hit in the throat by a shell fragment, this sergeant had had seven blood transfusions. Writing a note to his doctor, he asked, 'Will I live?' The doctor replied, 'Yes.' He wrote another note, asking, 'Will I be able to talk?' Again the answer was yes. He then wrote another note, saying, *'Then what in the hell am I worrying about?'*

Why don't you stop right now and ask yourself, 'What in the hell am I worrying about?' You will probably find that it is comparatively unimportant and insignificant.

About ninety per cent of the things in our lives are right and about ten per cent are wrong. If we want to be happy, all we have to do is to concentrate on the ninety per cent that are right and ignore the ten per cent that are wrong. If we want to be worried and bitter and have stomach ulcers, all we have to do is to concentrate on the ten per cent that are wrong and ignore the ninety per cent that are glorious.

The words 'Think and Thank' are inscribed in many of the Cromwellian churches of England. These words ought to be inscribed on our hearts, too, 'Think and Thank'. Think of all we have to be grateful for, and thank God for all our boons and bounties.

Jonathan Swift, author of *Gulliver's Travels,* was the most devastating pessimist in English literature. He was so sorry that he had been born that he wore black and fasted on his birthdays; yet, in his despair, this supreme pessimist of English literature praised the great health-giving powers of cheerfulness and happiness. 'The best doctors in the world,' he declared, 'are Doctor Diet, Doctor Quiet and Doctor Merryman.'

You and I may have the services of 'Doctor Merryman' free every hour of the day by keeping our attention fixed on all the incredible riches we possess—riches exceeding by far the fabled treasures of Ali Baba. Would you sell both your eyes for a billion dollars? What would you take for your two legs? Your hands? Your hearing? Your children? Your family? Add up your assets, and you will find that you won't sell what you have for all the gold ever amassed by the Rockefellers, the Fords and the Morgans combined.

But do we appreciate all this? Ah, no. As Schopenhauer said, 'We seldom think of what we have but always of what we lack.' Yes, the tendency to 'seldom think of what we have but always of what we lack' is the greatest tragedy on earth. It has probably caused more misery than all the wars and diseases in history.

Logan Pearsall Smith packed a lot of wisdom into a few words when he said, 'There are two things to aim at in life: first, to get what you want; and, after that, to enjoy it. Only the wisest of mankind achieve the second.'

Would you like to know how to make even dishwashing at the kitchen sink a thrilling experience? If so, read an inspiring book of incredible courage by Borghild Dahl. It is called *I Wanted to See.* You may borrow it from your public library or purchase it from your local bookstore or from the publisher, The Macmillan Company, 60 Fifth Avenue, New York City.

This book was written by a woman who was practically blind for half a century. 'I had only one eye,' she writes, 'and it was so covered with dense scars that I had to do all my seeing through one small opening in the left of the eye. I could see a book only by holding it up close to my face and by straining my one eye as hard as I could to the left.'

But she refused to be pitied, refused to be considered 'different'. As a child, she wanted to play hopscotch with other children, but she couldn't see the markings. So after the other children had gone home, she got down on the ground and crawled along with her eyes near to the marks. She memorized every bit of the ground where she and her friends played and soon became an expert at running games. She did her reading at home, holding a book of large print so close to her eyes that her eyelashes brushed the pages. She earned two college degrees: an B.A. from the University of Minnesota and a Master of Arts from Columbia University.

She started teaching in the tiny village of Twin Valley, Minnesota, and rose until she became professor of journalism and literature at Augustana College in Sioux Falls, South Dakota. She taught there for thirteen years, lecturing before women's clubs and giving radio talks about books and authors. 'In the back of my mind,' she writes, 'there had always lurked a fear of total blindness. In order to overcome this, I had adopted a cheerful, almost hilarious, attitude toward life.'

Then in 1943, when she was fifty-two years old, a miracle happened: an operation at the famous Mayo Clinic. She could now see forty times as well as she had ever been able to see before.

A new and exciting world of loveliness opened before her.

She now found it thrilling even to wash dishes in the kitchen sink. 'I begin to play with the white fluffy suds in the dishpan,' she writes. 'I dip my hands into them and I pick up a ball of tiny soap bubbles. I hold them up against the light, and in each of them I can see the brilliant colours of a miniature rainbow.'

As she looked through the window above the kitchen sink, she saw 'the flapping gray-black wings of the sparrows flying through the thick, falling snow.'

She found such ecstasy looking at the soap bubbles and sparrows that she closed her book with these words, '"Dear Lord," I whisper, "Our Father in Heaven, I thank Thee. I thank Thee."'

Imagine thanking God because you can wash dishes and see rainbows in bubbles and sparrows flying through the snow!

You and I ought to be ashamed of ourselves. All the days of our years we have been living in a fairyland of beauty, but we have been too blind to see, too satiated to enjoy.

POINTS TO REMEMBER:

1. Most of the things we worry over are insignificant.
2. Think and thank.
3. Focus on not what you don't have but on what you do.

19

EIGHT WORDS THAT CAN TRANSFORM YOUR LIFE

Yes, if we think happy thoughts, we will be happy. If we think miserable thoughts, we will be miserable. If we think fear thoughts, we will be fearful. If we think sickly thoughts, we will probably be ill. If we think failure, we will certainly fail. If we wallow in self-pity, everyone will want to shun us and avoid us. 'You are not,' said Norman Vincent Peale, 'you are not what you think you are; but what you *think*, you are.'

Am I advocating a habitual Pollyanna attitude toward all our problems? No, unfortunately, life isn't so simple as all that. But I am advocating that we assume a *positive* attitude instead of a negative attitude. In other words, we need to be concerned about our problems, but not worried. What is the difference between concern and worry? Let me illustrate. Every time I cross the traffic-jammed streets of New York, I am concerned about what I am doing—but not worried. Concern means realizing what the problems are, and calmly taking steps to meet them. Worrying means going around in maddening, futile circles.

A man can be concerned about his serious problems and still walk with his chin up and a carnation in his buttonhole.

Our mental attitude has an almost unbelievable effect even

on our physical powers. The famous British psychiatrist, J. A. Hadfield, gives a striking illustration of that fact in his splendid 54-page booklet: *The Psychology of Power*. 'I asked three men,' he writes, 'to submit themselves to test the effect of mental suggestion on their strength, which was measured by gripping a dynamometer.' He told them to grip the dynamometer with all their might. He had them do this under three different sets of conditions.

When he tested them under normal waking conditions, their average grip was 101 pounds.

When he tested them after he had hypnotized them and told them that they were very weak, they could grip only 29 pounds—less than a third of their normal strength. (One of these men was a prize fighter; and when he was told under hypnosis that he was weak, he remarked that his arm felt 'tiny, just like a baby's'.)

When Captain Hadfield then tested these men a third time, telling them under hypnosis that they were very strong, they were able to grip an average of 142 pounds. When their minds were filled with positive thoughts of strength, they increased their actual physical powers almost five hundred per cent.

Such is the incredible power of our mental attitude.

I am deeply convinced that our peace of mind and the joy we get out of living depends not on where we are, or what we have, or who we are, but solely upon our mental attitude. Outward conditions have very little to do with it.

Milton in his blindness discovered that same truth three hundred years ago,

'The mind is its own place, and in itself can make a heaven of hell, a hell of heaven.'

Napoleon and Helen Keller are perfect illustrations of Milton's statement: Napoleon had everything men usually crave—glory, power, riches—yet he said at Saint Helena, 'I have never known six happy days in my life'; while Helen Keller—blind, deaf, dumb—declared, 'I have found life so beautiful.'

If half a century of living has taught me anything at all, it has taught me that 'nothing can bring you peace but yourself.'

I am merely trying to repeat what Emerson said so well in the closing words of his essay on 'Self-Reliance', 'A political victory, a rise in rents, the recovery of your sick or the return of your absent friend, or some other quite external event, raises your spirits, and you think good days are preparing for you. Do not believe it. It can never be so. Nothing can bring you peace but yourself.'

Let me ask you a question: if merely acting cheerful and thinking positive thoughts of health and courage could save this man's life, why should you and I tolerate for one minute more our minor glooms and depressions? Why make ourselves, and everyone around us, unhappy and blue, when it is possible for us to start creating happiness by merely acting cheerful?

Years ago, I read a little book that had a lasting and profound effect on my life. It was called *As a Man Thinketh*, by James Allen, and here's what it said,

'A man will find that as he alters his thoughts towards things and other people, things and other people will alter towards him... Let a man radically alter his thoughts, and he will be astonished at the rapid transformation it will effect in the material conditions of his life. Men do not attract that which they want, but that which they are... The divinity that shapes our ends is in ourselves. It is our very self... All that a man achieves is the direct result of his own thoughts... A man can only rise, conquer and achieve by lifting up his thoughts. He can only remain weak and abject and miserable by refusing to lift up his thoughts.'

According to the book of Genesis, the Creator gave man dominion over the whole wide earth. A mighty big present. But I am not interested in any such super royal prerogatives. All I desire is dominion over myself—dominion over my thoughts; dominion over my fears; dominion over my mind and over my spirit. And the wonderful thing is that I know that I can attain this dominion to an astonishing degree, any time I want to, by merely controlling my actions—which in turn control my reactions.

So let us remember these words of William James, 'Much of what we call Evil...can often be converted into a bracing and tonic good by a simple change of the sufferer's inner attitude from one of fear to one of fight.'

Let's *fight* for our happiness!

POINTS TO REMEMBER:

1. If you think happy thoughts, you will be happy.
2. You are not what you think you are; but what you think, you are.
3. Our mental attitude also affects our physical powers.